The Dead Sea Scrolls The Gospel of Barnabas and The New Testament

M. A. Yusseff

American Trust Publications
10900 W. Washington Street
Indianapolis, Indiana 46231

Copyright © 1405 / 1985 American Trust Publications

All Rights Reserved

No part of this book may be reproduced by any means, nor translated into any other language, without prior written permission from the Publisher.

**Library of Congress Catalog Card No. 85-073210
ISBN No. 0-89259-061-0**

American Trust Publications
10900 W. Washington Street
Indianapolis, Indiana 46231 — USA

Tel: (317) 839-8150
Telex No: 276242 ISLAMIC BS

Printed in the United States of America

*Dedicated to the memory
of my parents
who nourished me
with love — spiritually,
materially,
and intellectually.*

CONTENTS

Preface i

Introduction — Jesus: A God or a Prophet iii
  M. Tariq Quraishi

The Discovery and Significance of the Scrolls 1
  Roots of Israelite Culture 2
  Israelite Opposition to Hellenization and
  the Essenes' Emergence 3
  The Nazerenes: A Sect of the Essenes 4
  Some Parallels between Essene and Nazarene Beliefs 7
  Thematic Coherence between the Gospel of Barnabas
  and Genuine Scholarship 10
  Jesus' Charge of corruption against the Jews 13
  Jesus' birth - the Reaffirmation of the Abrahamic Faith 14

The Dusk, The Beginning of the Age of the Gentiles 21
  The Waywardness of the Israelites 21
  The Minor Prophets 22
  Jesus' True Mission 24
  The Coming of the Gentiles 27
  The Third Empire 29
  The Fourth Empire 32

The Beginning of the anti-Christ Doctrine 35
  The Gentile Tendency to make men gods 35
  Jesus' warning that the Gentile would make Him a god 37
  The Trinity: a Pagan Expression 40
  Blasphemy and Division in Palestine 43
  Who were the Nicolaitans? 48
  The Origins of the Nicolaitan Heresy 51
  The Nicolaitan Heresy 54

The Gnostic Origin of the Christian Church 59
   The Ebionites as a sect distinct from the Nazarenes 59
   Ebionites' opposition to Paul the first Christian 61
   The Modernization of Paganism 65
   Paul's inadvertant admission that He
   was guilty of fabrication 69

The Formulation of the Greek Gospels 73
   Nazarene's opposition to Nicolaitan Heresy 73
   The Spurious nature of the Greek Gospels 79
   The Ceaseless corruption 81
   The Gospel of John - A Gnostic work 84

Is The Gospel of Barnabas the Original Source? 87
   Barnabas and the compilation of the Gospel 88
   Paul's decision to become a Nicolaitan 89
   Further evidence concerning the great antiquity of
   the Gospel of Barnabas 93
   The Jewish Rebellion, the anti-Semitism of the Gentiles
   and the survival of the Gospel of Barnabas 94
   The establishment of the Christian Church and
   the Nicolaitan Conspiracy 97

The Prophet Who was to Come 103
   Conflicting Messianic Prophecies at the time of Jesus 104
   The Harassment of the Nazarenes and Jesus' Prophecy about
   the coming Messiah 108
   The Messiah that Jesus spoke of 109
   A Messiah from the Ishmaelites 111
   Evidence from beyond Israel 115
   Hiding the Truth behind the double Meaning 116
   The esoteric (hidden) meaning 117

Appendix
   List of Biblical Authorities 125

Index 129

PREFACE

As far back as 1961, I became aware of the Essenes as one who best fitted the description of the people of the Qumran (Dead Sea) Scrolls. Over the years while reading a number of scholarly works on the Scrolls and the Essenes, I became familiar with Essenic terminology. One day when I came across a copy of *The Gospel of Barnabas*, the abundance of Essenic terminology in its text struck me with a sense of discovery — a discovery I wanted to share with others. If its critics were right, how could this gospel account of Jesus' life and ministry read so much, in its expression, like the work of one accustomed to using and thinking in Essenic concepts and terminology? How could this be unless the biblical scholars who felt that there was some connection between the Nazarenes and the Essenes were right. Drawing upon my research training, I set about analyzing *The Gospel of Barnabas* from a historical perspective and compared it with the Qumran Scrolls for terminology and similarity of thought.

This work is the first of a series of works based on a scientific approach to discern the truth. Too bad the critics of this astonishing document — to my knowledge — have been overly biased and dedicated to the blind defense of their particular system of religious beliefs that certain statements in the text of the Gospel, which on the surface appear to be suspect, have been seized upon in an effort to discredit this amazing document. My own religious belief stand on its own, with, or without, *The Gospel of Barnabas*, in light of scientific investigation. Therefore, there is no reason for me to fall into this same kind of erroneous thinking in analyzing this ancient work. Let us pursue the "truth" and leave the indifferent to themselves.

M.A. Yusseff
January, 1986

Introduction

JESUS: A GOD OR A PROPHET?

Whether *The Gospel of Barnabas* is genuine or not is a question tied to another question — whether Jesus is God incarnate or not. For if Jesus is not God, then the present gospels of the New Testament fall apart and the search for an authentic gospel becomes inevitable.

To begin with, Jesus' humanity is not a new issue that arose with the modern criticism of the biblical texts or with the rise of Islam. The history of Christianity is rife with such discussions. Nor has there been a dearth of such Christians who dared to deny Jesus' divinity and then were silenced by death or by a vehment charge of heresy. One need not delve far back into the Christian past for its intolerance to this aspect of christology. As early as 1546 in Munster, Holland, 30,000 people were put to death because they denied Jesus' divinity.[1] Only eight years ago, Professor Robert Alley was sacked from the chairmanship of the Department of Religion, University of Richmond (Virginia), because he denied that Jesus ever claimed to be the Son of God.[2] Times have changed, otherwise he would have lost his head — something that Rev. John Gray the leader of Scotland's Presbyterian Church could not resist saying on the publication of John Hick's *The Myth of God Incarnate* in July 1977: "If the authors were honorable, they would have resigned their professorship of theology and divest themselves of their status as Christian ministers... In a more militant age I would not have bothered myself with mere words. I would have laid a charge of heresy."[3]

No wonder during the last 1600 years or so *The Gospel of Barnabas* was first anathematized and later forced out of circulation for its alleged heresy.

---

[1] Earl Morse Wilbur, *A History of Unitarianism — Socianianism and its Antecedents,* Beacon Press, Boston, 1945, p.41.
[2] *The Washington Post,* January 5, 1978 and *Islamic Horizons,* March 1978.
[3] *The International Tribune,* July 1977.

Ironically, modern criticism of the biblical texts is more or less supportive of what *The Gospel of Barnabas* has been saying all along — that Jesus is not a God or the Son of God, but a true and great prophet of God in the tradition of the Old Testament. This criticism or the resultant theology does not go beyond the New Testament. Rather it seeks justification from it.

One can develop a number of approaches from this criticism of the biblical texts for what may be considered to be a search for the real Jesus.

Approach (a) attempts to unravel the mystery surrounding Jesus by evaluating the evidence about Jesus as a man and as a God. According to this approach, which uses the biblical text for building up the case against Jesus as God, there are two trends in the New Testament — the minor and the dominant trends. The minor trend, which does not come from Jesus, has been blown out of proportion to support his divinity, while the dominant one, which comes directly from Jesus, denies his godhood.

The minor trend in the gospels derives its support from Titus 2:13; John 8:58; 10:30,33; 20:28. Biblical scholars such as James Barr however discount their clarity. For example of John 10:30, his views are:

> When Jesus says in John 10:30 that he and the Father are "one," he does so in the context of numerous other sayings which make it clear that this does not betoken congruence and identity.[4]

The dominant trend stands on Mark 5:6; 3:11; 10:17-18; 15:39; 12:29: Matthew 22:37 and John 10:34, where Jesus often directly and sometimes indirectly denies his godhood. Concluding his theme, James Barr says:

> ... at least in these Gospels Jesus is not depicted as presenting himself directly as one who is God. He presents himself much more by the use of the enigmatic term "Son of Man." It is others, and not mainly himself, who designate him as "Son of God," and even these mainly either (a) among those who reject his authority or (b) who speak after his crucifixion ... In the Gospels the stress lies on Jesus fulfilling his mission, on the question whether and how he is Messiah of Israel: and only secondarily is his character and person verbalized through identification as Son of God or as God.[5]

---

[4] James Barr, *Beyond Fundamentalism*, The Westminister Press, Philadelphia, 1984, p. 57.
[5] Ibid., pp. 58, 59.

Approach (b) to find out the real Jesus is based on the Old Testament. For if the Old Testament is part of the Bible, then any concept derived from the New Testament must have its support from the Old Testament. This approach is grounded in Jesus' saying that "Scripture cannot be broken." This is especially true of terms like "Son of God" which are embedded in the Hebrew tradition. According to this approach, the expression "Son of God" is at best metaphorical and is often used for pious people, heavenly, angelic beings and kings. For example, 11 Samuel 7:14 and Psalms 2:7 use it for ideal king-Messiah. Psalms 82:1, 6-7 refers to prophets as gods and "sons of the Most High":

> God has taken his place in the divine council; in the midst of the gods he holds judgment... I say, "You are gods, sons of the Most High, all of you; nevertheless, you shall die like men, and fall like any prince."

It was to this passage from the Old Testament that Jesus is said to have referred to in John 10:34:

> Jesus answered them (in response to the charge of blasphemy by the Jews), 'Is it not written in your law, "I said you are gods?" If he called them gods to whom the word of God came (and Scripture cannot be broken), do you say of him whom the Father consecrated and sent to the world, "You are blaspheming," because I said, "I am the son of God"'

Approach (c) probes into the pre-Christian environment to see to what intent and purpose and for what kind of people the term God was used. If it is proven that such an expression was in vogue at that time, then the divinity invested in Jesus has to be understood in that sense.

There are innumerable instances of such usage in pre and post-crucifixion eras, but for the sake of brevity we will take only a few.

The Greek philosopher Pythagoras was said to have been the incarnate son of Hermes, who appeared to many and came to heal men. We have on the authority of Plutarch that Plato had a miraculous birth:

> I do not find it strange if it is not by a physical approach, like a man's, but some other kind of contact or touch, by other agencies, that a god alters mortal nature and makes it pregnant with a more divine offspring... In general (the Egyptians) allow

vi   Introduction

sexual intercourse with a mortal woman to a male god...[6]

In fact, Plutarch's *Lives* is full of biographies about men who had divine genealogies.

The Roman Emperor Augustus, whose reign saw the birth of Jesus, was portrayed as god, Mercury incarnate. In his *Ode to Augustus,* Horace says:

> Whom of the gods shall the people summon to the needs of the falling Empire... To whom shall Jupitor assign the task of expiating guilt? ...With form changed may you ... appear on earth ... late you may return to the skies.[7]

The Jewish literature is also not free of such flights of imagination. Some rabbinic traditions say that Moses along with Enoch and Elijah went alive to heaven. It is also suggested that he transformed into an angel. In 11 Kings 2:1, we find Elijah ascending to heaven by chariot of fire and whirlwind.

In the post-crucifixion era, we find the absurd case of Bishop Eusebius "who saw the hand of providence at work when he heralded Constantine as almost a new manifestation of the Logos bringing the kingdom of God on earth."[8] Needless to say, Bishop Eusebius was a leading Christian who was glorifying an emperor in the same language that the writers of gospels had used for Jesus — an interesting insight into the Christian mind so willing to see anyone out of the ordinary as a manifestation of God.

Approach (d) in quest of the real Jesus could be called the Samaritan hypothesis. According to this approach, developed by Professor Michael Goulder, the genesis of Jesus' divinity as an idea can be traced to Samaritan theology with which earlier Christianity had an encounter. Such a hypothesis views the New Testament documents portraying a dialectic, "in which the primitive eschatological gospel reached a synthesis with just such a position."[9]

The Samaritans were half Jewish in their beliefs. In their traditions Simon is a legend who along with others became Christian. This Simon, Justin says, was "native of the village Gitto, who in the reign of Claudius Caesar did mighty acts of magic. He was considered a god... and almost all the

---

[6] Frances Young, "Two Roots or a Tangled Mass?" in John Hick's *The Myth of God Incarnate,* The Westminster Press, Philadelphia, 1977, p. 95.

[7] Ibid., p. 97. Horace, *Odes*, 1. 2.

[8] Frances Young, "A Cloud of Witness" Loc. cit., p. 29.

[9] Michael Goulden, "The Two Roots of the Christian Myth," loc. cit., p. 68.

Samaritans, and a few even of other nations, worship him, and acknowledge him as the first God." This man-god, according to their theology, stood by God who descended for him in the clouds. Their faith in dualism and incarnation notwithstanding, the Samaritans did not believe in the resurrection of the dead. They believed instead in a final age of God's good pleasure, when a "prophet like unto Moses" would come. In order to assimilate the Samaritans into Christianity, says Michael Goulder, the writers of the New Testament responded in the following manner:

> The great power has come in the form of Jesus to reveal the truth, to give us knowledge of the Divine One. Through him, and through the Gerizim traditions, we know what lies behind the universe ... With his coming the age of good pleasure has been inaugurated ... We have seen in him the Prophet like unto Moses who has instituted a new commandment.[10]

The New Testament shows a progressive assimilation of the Samaritan theology. "One of Paul's most admirable qualities," says Michael Goulder, "is his flexibilty, his ability to steal the opposition's clothes while they are bathing." The truth of this statement can be seen in 1 Corinthians 1-3; 8:1,7,10,11; 11 Corinthians 2:14; 4:6; 6:6; 8:7; 10:5; 11:6 and Ephesians 1:9,17; 3:3. Professor Goulder illustrates his point by saying that "the verbs *oida* and *ginoska* hardly occur in the Synoptics, but both come more than fifty times in John — a far cry from 1 Corinthians." By the time Romans 1:3 is written, Paul fully embraces the idea.[11]

Approach (e) toward discovering the real Jesus is based on the premise that there are two phases of christology. One relates to the earliest when Jesus was alive, untouched by the writers' desire to create a larger-than-life portrait of him. This Jesus is thrust into our consciousness as a prophet of God who has come to warn and give the glad tidings to those who will submit themselves to God. The second phase relates to later times — long after his death — when title after title is given to him mostly as part of the evangelists' effort to win over a particular audience.

This approach first refurbishes the image of a prophet, because to an ordinary church-going Christian the title conjures up in his mind some kind of a soothsayer or a foreteller. Addressing this mentality, Professor Morton Scott Enslin says that "the Semitic prophet was regarded, and

---

[10] Ibid., p. 75.
[11] Ibid., p. 77.

regarded himself, as definitely seized by the divine spirit and subject to it. Thus the word prophet was understood in the sense of forthteller, that is, one speaking for another. Indeed the Hebrew word *nabi* has been considered by some Semitists as the passive of the verb meaning "to enter," and thus the "entered one." Whether this derivative be etymologically correct or not, it emphasizes precisely the Semitic view."[12] That is why Jesus' opponents thought he was possessed by an evil spirit.

As to Jesus' prophethood, which is the pre-crucifixion phase of christology, we are led to a scene in Mark 6:1-4 where Jesus is shown to have come back to Nazareth. He begins his ministry. People are astonished at the words of wisdom from his mouth, saying, "Where did this man get these things ... Is this not the carpenter the son of Mary?... The curiosity was justified and if they took offense that too was justified because they knew him as one of their own. Here in one of those revealing passages Jesus is shown to be hurt by their lack of understanding his role as a God-sent Prophet and says: "A prophet is not without honor except in his own country, among his own relatives, and in his own house."

Again when according to Luke 13:33, Jesus is informed that Herod might kill him, he observes: "... for it cannot be that a prophet perish out of Jerusalem." We have this same impression from the people who are reported to have been talking about Jesus after his death. In another scene from Luke 24:19, we are introduced to Cleopas who on the face of evidence can be said to be someone close enough to know Jesus or someone whom Luke knew (if there is any such probability) responding to a stranger's inquiry (who happens by some bizarre twist to be Jesus himself and they do not recognize him) ... "The things concerning Jesus of Nazareth, who was a *Prophet mighty* in *deed* and *word* before God and all the people."

That Jesus was a prophet can also be seen in Luke's very moving story of the anointing of Jesus by the sinful woman. After she finishes anointing him, the Pharisee who is Jesus' host at dinner says: "This man, if he were a prophet, would have perceived who and what manner of woman this is that touches him, that she is a sinner." The Pharisee's taunting remarks would have made no sense if Jesus had not been known as a Prophet.

Even when scribes and Pharisees ask for a sign from him, they address him as "teacher." The implications are very clear: Jesus had identified himself as a prophet of God and as a proof they were asking for a sign. Equally revealing is his response to them. He equates himself with another

---

[12]Morton Scott Enslin, *The Prophet from Nazareth*, McGraw Hill Book Company, Inc. New York, 1961, pp. 66-67.

Israelite prophet such as Jonah. "For as Jonah was three days and three nights in the belly of the great fish, so will be the Son of Man..." This passage appears to be an interpolation on two grounds. First, the God incarnate compares himself to Jonah who is a prophet and a man. Second, the sign is asked for the immediate now and not in the future. Nevertheless, this reference to an earlier prophet is not a coincidence but more or less a continuing theme in the gospels. In Matthew 17:1-8, readers are taken to a mountain. Accompanying Jesus are three of his close companions. Suddenly they see Jesus' face changing into a shining sun. At this point Peter suggests: "Lord, it is good for us to be here; if you wish, let us make here three tabernacles: one for you, one for Moses, and one for Elijah." Why did Peter talk about Moses and Elijah, and why did both of them later show up on the mountain is a valid point of inquiry. Whatever the authenticity of the scene, it suggests three prophets come together. Again in Acts 3:22-26, where Peter is shown speaking to "men of Israel," we have a very clear statement from his lips: "For Moses truly said to the fathers, 'The Lord your God will raise up for you a *Prophet like me* from your *brethren'*..." To you first, God having raised up *His servant Jesus* sent Him to bless you..."

Obviously, all these approaches to the study of the biblical texts reveal Jesus to be no other than a man, though in the mold of a great prophet. If certain passages in the New Testament project Jesus as God, then it is a Greek god, built by the writers to evangelize an audience which lived in a god-complex environment. At the same time, these approaches are based on the premise that the Bible is not the word of God but the product of the evangelists' mind. As Ralph P. Martin says in his *Reconciliation — A Study of Paul's Theology*. "They (the gospels) contain interpreted history, expressed and angled so as to enforce the Church's claim that, in Jesus of Nazareth, God was personally present in a new way, and that in the now exalted 'Lord' he offers his salvation, wrought out in the historical ministry of Jesus to all."[13]

If that is the case, what is *The Gospel of Barnabas* status as compared to the New Testament. Many cases can be built from the two to establish the former's truthfulness and the latter's syncretic character.

To begin with, *The Gospel of Barnabas* is harmonious in its doctrine and as such, in line with the Hebrew tradition. Its hard-core monotheism is easy to understand and does not bring the reader to a point of desperation

---

[13] Ralph P. Martin, *Reconciliation — A Study of Paul's Theology*, John Knox Press, Atlanta, 1981, p. 203.

or mental exhaustion to end up with a sigh, "God is a mystery!" Added to this, its principal character does not emit fire from his mouth nor curse anyone the way he does in the New Testament. Jesus of *The Gospel of Barnabas* is a genuine person, deeply concerned over the fall of man. He is aware of his place in the cosmos. That is why overwhelmed by the majesty of his Creator, he serves His cause diligently without any fear. His wisdom is prophetic and his character consistent — a far cry from the Jesus of the New Testament who talks in parables and contradicts himself every now and then.

A scene from Matthew 16:13-23 will illustrate the point:

> When Jesus came into the region of Caesarea Philippi, He asked His disciples, saying, "Who do men say that I, the Son of Man, am?"
>
> So they said, "Some say John the Baptist, some Elijah, and others Jeremiah or one of the prophets."
>
> He said to them, "But who do you say that I am?"
>
> And Simon Peter answered and said, "You are the the Son of the living God."
>
> Jesus answered and said to him, "Blessed are you, Simon Bar-Jonah, for flesh and blood has not *revealed this* to you *but My Father* who is in heaven.
>
> "And I also say to you that you are *Peter,* and on this *rock I will build My church,* and the gates of Hades shall not prevail against it.
>
> "And I will give you *the keys of the kingdom of heaven,* and whatever you bind on earth will be bound in heaven, and whatever you loose on earth will be loosed in heaven."
>
> Then He commanded His disciples that they should tell no one that He was Jesus the Christ.
>
> From that time Jesus began to show to His disciples that He must go to Jerusalem, and suffer many things from the elders and chief priests and scribes, and be killed, and be raised again the third day.
>
> Then Peter took Him aside and began to rebuke Him, saying "Far be it from You, Lord; this shall not happen to You!"
>
> But He turned and said to Peter, "Get behind Me, *Satan! You are an offense to Me,* for you are not mindful of the things of God, but the things of men."
>
> Then Jesus said to His disciples, "If anyone desires to come after Me, let him deny himself, and take up his cross, and follow Me.

"For whoever desires to save his life will lose it, and whoever loses his life for My sake will find it.

"For what is a man profited if he gains the whole world, and loses his own soul? Or what will a man give in exchange for his soul?"

The preceding passage from Matthew has the following elements:

Jesus wants to know what people think about him.

He is told people think he is either John the Baptist or Elijah or one of the prophets.

Peter's assessment of Jesus is that he is Christ the Son of the living God.

This elevates Peter's position because he is the recipient of revelation from God. He gets the keys of the kingdom of heaven.

Jesus does not want his disciples to let anyone know that he was Christ.

At no point does Jesus contradict his disciples about what people think of him. He is certainly not John, nor is he Elijah or Jeremiah. He could have told them in an unambiguous way about his self. Instead, he turns to Peter. And when Peter tells him "he is Christ the Son of the living God" — an expression commonly used for people of exceptional moral and political abilities, he elevates Peter by giving him the key to the kingdom of heaven on earth.

But in the same flow of events Jesus calls the same dignified Peter "Satan" and an "offense" to him. At least two objections can be raised to this whole episode:

1) Why would Jesus like to conceal his identity as "Christ," especially when he has been sent by "the Father" to absolve people of their sins? Was he supposed to lead his life incognito? Would it help his mission? Was he not supposed to establish a role model for his followers?

2) What was Peter's sin that it warranted an extremely harsh name "Satan" for him? Is not Satan the symbol of everything evil? After all Peter, like a devoted follower who loved his master, only desired that he is not harmed, "Far be it from you, Lord." Does his love for him constitute such a grave sin that it makes Jesus flare up? Where is Jesus' loving disposition? Or is he a kind of a master who knows not how to respond to his followers' love for him?

No matter how best an interpretation is given to this sudden shift in

Jesus' mood, sophistry will not help salvage his character. The biblical Jesus in this scene has no redeeming feature — his character is badly distorted. The irony is unmistakable: the God incarnate who wants to die in order to save others has no disposition to bear with a disciple's love. He could have told Peter with the same love that Peter had shown for him that "no my friend I have to die." After all, Peter was not using violence to stop him. Obviously, there is something missing in this passage from Matthew. It is possible that either Jesus did not use the word Satan for Peter, or he did use it but the context is different. Perhaps Peter said something sacrilegious that called for such a stern reaction from Jesus — we do not know from this gospel.

Some biblical scholars such as Dr. Enslin view Matthew 13:18 — "And I also say to you that you are Peter, and on this rock I will build My church..." a later addition and "improbable as genuine words of Jesus." He says in the whole gospel tradition the word church occurs twice to justify the existence of the Church separate from the Jewish synagogue — "in deliberate opposition to the later claims of Jerusalem for pre-eminence because their leader was James, the brother of Jesus."[14]

But this interpolation is minor as compared to the deliberate attempt of the gospel's writers to graft Jesus as a Savior on the readers' mind. That in the process Jesus' nobility has been compromised is of little concern to them.

For the sake of argument one can say what kind of God is Jesus that he does not know the psyche of Peter — in the same breath he is blessed, a recipient of special knowledge from "the Father" and then moments later an accursed being, a "Satan." This is too great a paradox to be glossed over. In portraying Jesus as a Savior and a God, the gospel ends up assassinating his character.

So obvious are the problems with this passage that honest biblical scholarship is forced to take note of it. "We must not assume," says *The Interpreter's Dictionary of the Bible*, "that these verses necessarily belong in the context where we now find them. Form criticism has made it clear that the gospel tradition was preserved at first mainly in the form of separate units; single incidents, sayings, or parables were repeatedly used in the life of the church to serve its needs. Even though a general outline of Jesus' life was preserved, the exact situation in which a saying was spoken by Jesus was often unknown. Our gospel writers therefore had to organize their material in a form more unified than the oral tradition had. And of all

---

[14] Morton Scott Enslin, loc. cit., p. 165.

the gospel writers, the writer of Matthew is most clearly skilled in organizing sayings of Jesus in large discourses."[15] How skillful is Matthew, we leave it to the readers' judgment.

Contrary to this, *The Gospel of Barnabas* gives the same episode in a far more natural way that exalts Jesus as well as his disciples.

Barnabas first sets the scene: There are conjectures about the person of Jesus. His miracles are causing a problem of perception for the common men. As a human being, Peter is also for a while influenced by the giddy events of the past few days, and in a moment of blurred understanding he commits his life's worst crime — maybe his master is Messiah the *Son of God*. Jesus, of course, should be upset with this utterance. His own disciple is guilty of blasphemy of the highest order — an offense that can be committed by a devil only and none else. But declaring Peter as devil is not anticlimactic to his exaltation as a blessed one with the key of the kingdom of heaven on earth in the Matthian sense. Nowhere does Jesus' character come close to Matthew's absurd figure. Peter's character is also understandable — a true disciple who offends his master but then out of remorse cries and asks for forgiveness. Matthew's narrative lacks this very important dimension of both Jesus and Peter's personalities. What follows is equally enlightening, and heightens the role of Jesus as a reformer. His discourse on the majesty of God and His uniqueness sharpens his listeners' consciousness of Him. "If our God willed not to show himself to Moses His servant, nor to Elijah whom He also loved, nor to any prophet, do you think that God should show Himself to this faithless generation." In these few words, he demolishes all the myths built around him. The greatness and the uniqueness of God come to the fore. His summation is a piece of rhetoric that goes deep into one's soul and in response the soul gives up to the greatness of its Creator. "But know you not that God created all things of nothing with a single word, and all men have their origin out of a piece of clay? Now, how shall God have a likeness to man."

Doubtless, in its monotheistic theme and genuineness of Jesus' character, *The Gospel of Barnabas* has no peers in the gospel literature.

As to Yusseff's book, it does a commendable job of authenticating *The Gospel of Barnabas* and in the process opens up an entirely new field of research. The Dead Sea Scrolls, ever since their discovery in 1947, have meant many things to many. Contrary to evangelists' claims, their discovery has brought no meaningful evidence to strengthen traditional Christianity based on the New Testament. The evidence presented so far is

---

[15] *The Interpreter's Dictionary of the Bible*, Abingdon Press, New York, 1962, p. 752.

of a dubious nature and the rationale is flimsy to say the least. For example, Manfred Barthel's *What the Bible Really Says* is jubilant over the discovery of the Dead Sea Scrolls, and makes sweeping statements about the remarkable parallels between the gospels and the Qumran Scrolls. But these parallels ironically do not exceed beyond three quotes from John and two from the Qumran's. For example, the Qumran Scrolls talk about the conflict between light and darkness. This, Barthel says, is the source of the Essene version of "Blessed are the poor in spirit."[16] However, this same parallel is objected to by Antony Newcombe Gilkes in his *The Impact of the Dead Sea Scrolls* on grounds that "Christ rejected all physical violence as a policy... But the Covenanters were brought up on the war of the Sons of the Light..."[17]

In order to establish the link between the gospels and the Scrolls, Barthel refers to John 1:4 — "In Him (God) was life; and the life was the light of men," followed by John 8:12 — "I am the light of the world: he that followeth me shall not walk in darkness, but shall have the light of life." Both are statements of universal truth, and other religions in other times have also spoken of it. Yet Barthel sees a parallel between the two.

Of John and the Qumran's, he says: "It is not always easy to tell the difference between John, who is writing in his Greek philosophical vein at least, and the Essenes: "It is God who has established all things, and without Him nothing comes to pass (Qumran Texts)." And "all things were made by him; and without him was not anything made that was made (John 1:3)."[18]

Again, both statements are general in their import and any religion worth the name will regard them as self-evident truth. A parallel is meaningful only if it is drawn between the specifics and not the generalities. But Barthel likes to do so. Whether there is anything in the Scrolls that authenticates the doctrine of Trinity or a Savior-Messiah of the New Testament, such writings would not even give a whisper. For example, the Qumran Scrolls do mention that even in the first century BC, titles such as the Son of God and Son of the Most High were used for some human being of that era:

> ...*But your son* shall be great upon the earth *O King! All (men) shall make peace,* and all shall serve *him. He shall be called the*

---

[16] Manfred Barthel, *What the Bible Really Says*, Bell Publishing Company, New York, 1980, p. 285.

[17] Antony N. Silkes, *The Impact of the Dead Sea Scrolls*, Macmillan and Company, New York, 1962, p. 137.

[18] Manfred Barthel, loc. cit., p. 285.

son of the Great God, and by his name shall he be named. He shall be hailed (as) the Son of God, and they shall call him the Son of the Most High.[19]

But writers like Barthel and Antony Newcombe Gilkes would not like others to reflect upon the implications of such passages from the Scrolls, because this will invalidate their cherished doctrine of Jesus' divinity.

On the other hand, Yusseff's work brings out striking similarities between *The Gospel of Barnabas* and the Scrolls by showing that both Jesus and the Penitents of the Qumran were the followers of the Abrahamic faith; though Jesus remains to be a better follower, for he received revelation. This continuity of the monotheistic theme in the two documents, despite the Penitents' reliance on the Jewish books of the Old Testament, which were doubtlessly corrupted, is far more important than talking about God who established (made) all things.

That in this exercise to search for the true Gospel of Jesus the New Testament comes out badly bruised, is not Yusseff's fault. On this count, he is in the company of a galaxy of biblical scholars who unequivocally corroborate him.

According to Yusseff's thesis, Jesus' coming did not call for the abolition of the Abrahamic faith or the institution of a new faith based on the vicarious sacrifice of a man-god. He consistently maintains that Jesus is a link in the continuation of the Hebrew tradition. This is an exceedingly important point because until his coming, the Abrahamic faith was confined to the narrow racial and parochial concerns of the Israelites. Jesus broadened their concerns and diluted their rigid confines. That this led to termination of the Israelite dispensation was inevitable. But universalizing the Abrahamic tradition by enlarging upon its laws was left to another son of Abraham, Muhammad.

M. Tariq Quraishi
January 14, 1986

---

[19] J.A. Fitzmyer, "The Contribution of Qumran Aramaic to the Study of the New Testament," *New Testament Studies*, vol. 20, 1974, pp. 382-407. The italicized words are said to be fragmented in the Scrolls.

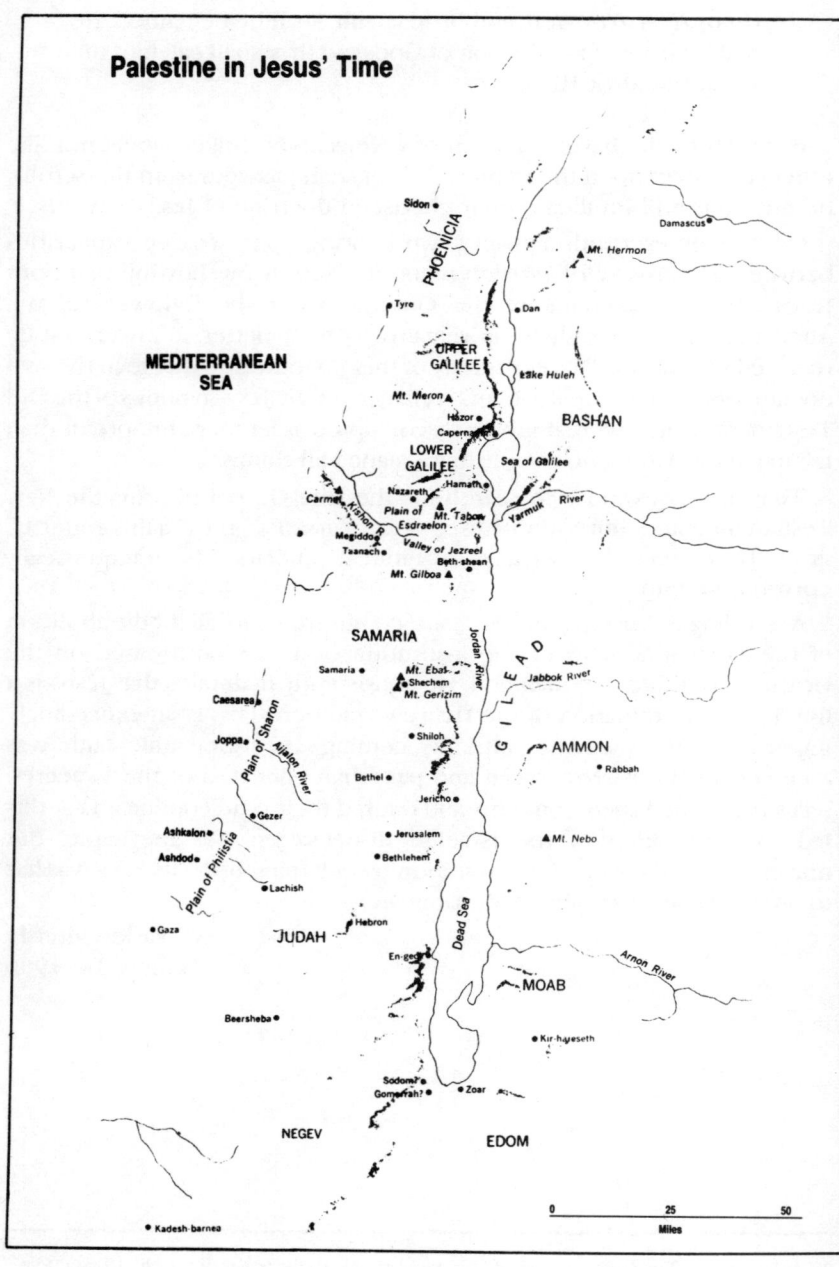

THE DISCOVERY AND SIGNIFICANCE OF THE SCROLLS

In the summer of 1947, an Ishmaelite shepherd discovered manuscripts of the book of Isaiah in a cave near the Dead Sea. The manuscripts were found to be about a thousand years older than any previously known copies of the Torah (five books of Moses) and the Prophets. Further discoveries revealed other manuscripts now collectively known as the "Qumran Scrolls" (or the Dead Sea Scrolls).

The Scrolls formed the literature of an Essene community reported to have lived on the Dead Sea's western shore, a few miles south of Jericho. Historically, their time coincides with John the Baptist. It is because of this, and their contents, that the Scrolls are considered to be of great importance to the study of the Nazarene Movement once headed by Jesus the Nazarene. It is believed that whereas the "Scrolls" were peculiar to the Qumran community, they must have been used by the Essene movement as a whole.

The Qumran Scrolls introduce us to a segment of the overall religious reformation movement of the Jews, which looked upon itself as the true and ideal congregation of Israel. They also believed themselves to be the remnant of Jews who, like the Rechabites of Ishmael's seed, had remained faithful to the Abrahamic Covenant with God. In their view, this insured their continuance as a people. It was only by a succession of such pious "remnants" that the Covenant, they believed, had been upheld in the Israelite history.

Among the Qumran Scrolls there is one known as the Damascus Document, which says that in the early history of the Qumran community, the Penitents of Israel left the land of Judea and settled in the land of Damascus temporarily. Here, in their attempt to separate themselves from the unrighteous, they entered into a "New Covenant" spoken of in the book of Jeremiah (Jeremiah 31:31). Settlements of such penitents also existed in Galilee, Decapolis, Gilead, Bashan, the areas of Gaulan and Hauran and on the way toward Lebanon and Damascus.

These communities thought of themselves as following in the footsteps of their forefathers, who were led out of Egypt by the Prophet Moses. The Penitents' exodus was their withdrawal from their cities and villages into the wilderness. What they envisaged, however, was not relinquishing the Abrahamic Covenant, which was upheld by the Mosaic law, nor its substitution with Graeco-Roman philosophy or theology, but a new affirmation of it. In short, they wanted to return to a purer form of the Abrahamic religion.

Roots of Israelite Culture

An awareness of the Arabian roots of the Israelites is important if one is to understand their spirituality and the motivation to extirpate the anti-Judaic presence of Hellenism from their land.

The German orientalist, Hugo Winkler, after recounting the three civilizations which exerted a great influence on the Bible (the Babylonian, the Egyptian, and the Anatolian), rightly points out: "The Arabic field can be included with those other three as the fourth center of culture. If we see in Arabia the home of the Semitic peoples, to which Israel also belongs, we must expect that all that can be established concerning the life and character of Arabian people is fitted to disclose to us Israel's life and thought in its primitive conditions." Ditlef Nielsen, the Scandinavian scholar says: "The Hebrews alone among the Semites have preserved in the legends of the Patriarchs and Moses a tradition of the earlier Bedawi (Bedouin) life and the entrance into a land of civilization."[1] He says further that "the central nerve of the Hebrew religion leads back to old Arabia," a statement of fact in which the word "religion" denotes the most extensive and vitally important aspect of Israel's history.[2]

European opposition to recognizing the Arabian roots of the Israelite nation and its spiritual way of life is based not on facts, but on a desire to perpetuate in their own minds, and in the minds of others, the misconception that Graeco-Roman speculation, which so characterizes their idea of religion, is the legitimate successor to the Abrahamic religion. Such a view implies that the Abrahamic religion was supposed to be replaced, which, in fact, was not the case (Genesis 22:18). Both the Ishmaelites and the Israelites were to be the initial bearers of God's word, though it was predestined to go beyond these two people in order to bring about a greater spiritual nation of believers from all over the world. This is the all-important meaning of Genesis 22:18, read with Genesis 17:9-13.

---

[1] James Allen Montgomery, *Arabia and The Bible*, KATV Publishing House Inc., 1969, pp. 4-5.
[2] Ibid.

This is also one of the most important themes presented in the authentic Gospel preached by Jesus, and *not* Paul, and recorded by Matthew and Barnabas, and compiled by the latter.

Israelite Opposition to Hellenization and the Essenes' Emergence

The Essene movement is a part of Israel's history and came into being as a reaction to the Hellenists' attempt to Hellenize the Israelites.

Palestine opened up to Hellenization in the early days of Alexander's (356-323 BC) campaign to Hellenize the world. With Jewish adherence to Abrahamic faith still strong, Palestine was not responsive to Hellenism. Nevertheless, by 175 BC, when Antiochus ascended the throne of his portion of what had been Alexander's empire, the Jewish community was already deeply divided. There was a strong group of Hellenized Jews who used their influence to promote the idea that since Hellenism was everywhere gaining ground, Judaism must abandon those things which set it apart (the weekly day of rest, circumcision, abstinence from certain foods and so on), in order to have a place in the emerging new world.[3]

With the appearance of such Hellenized souls, we may well have the earliest emergence among Jews of what was to become part of the Nicolaitan heresy. In 168 BC, a Jewish revolt in opposition to the Hellenization imposed by Antiochus Epiphanes, ruler of the Seleucid dynasty of Syria, broke out. The leaders of this revolt were the Maccabees (Hasmoneans). A graphic account of this historic episode is given in the First Book of the Maccabees. Suffice it to say here that the non-conformists gathered in the Judean wilderness southeast of Jerusalem. Their refusal to engage their enemy on the Sabbath resulted in a frightful massacre. When news of the massacre reached Matthias, who was wiser in law than those slain and was willing to fight on the Sabbath, he formed a guerilla army with the Hasideans (the faithful). The Jews who declined to join them were struck down as enemies, while others managed to flee to the Gentiles. The loyal freedom fighters, or terrorists depending on one's point of view, destroyed pagan altars, and circumcised the uncircumcised. By 165 BC, the Hasideans (Hasidim) had achieved a costly victory and were able to rededicate a cleansed "Temple of the Lord" to the worship of God: they threw out the heathen alter of Zeus, which Antiochus had erected there three years ago.

---

[3]L.H. Grollenberg, *Atlas of the Bible*, trans. Joyce M.H. Reid, Thomas Nilson and Sons, New York, 1956, pp. 109-110.

But there were people among the inhabitants of Palestine who realized that the Maccabean victories were at best a "little help," as the book of Daniel calls them — a slight therapy for a sickness (Hellenism) that went far deeper. Then there were those who felt that the universal law of cause and effect was operating in the events they were witnessing. To them, the persecution of the people by Antiochus was a divine chastisement for their usurpation of the Covenant. What God required of the descendants of Abraham, both Ishmaelites and Israelites, was not burnt sacrifices, but true repentance. There were many among them who had left Jerusalem and its corrupted condition prior to 168 BC, because they thought it would be better to starve to death in the desert than to deny God and starve spiritually in the flesh-pots of Jerusalem. Such people came to be known as the Essenes. Their ascetic way of life was inspired by the "old Arabian lifestyle" of the Patriachs, which was so sternly upheld by the Rechabites.

The Nazarenes: A sect of the Essenes

Abraham, the Patriarch of the Arabs and Jews, and the spiritual father of the true worshippers of the God of Abraham, has long been acknowledged by scholars in various parts of the world as having been an Arab sheikh. Doubtless, his dignity and manners exemplify the courtesy and self-possession of an Arab chieftain. The same is true of Ishmael, Isaac, and Jacob.

In the forty-year wanderings of the Israelites, Moses molded the Jewish clans into a united tribal nation on the advice of his Arabian father-in-law Jethro (Exodus 18:5-24). This advice, along with their experience in the desert, contributed to the molding of Israel and its consciousness as a nation. This experience in the desert was the classical age of Israel's spiritual life. It was the spirit of this classical age that the Essenes were trying to recapture. The Prophet Amos considered it as one of the great acts of God (Amos 2:10, 5:25; Hosea 2:16, 12:10; Jeremiah 2:2).

As stated, the Damascus Document relates how in the early history of the Qumran community "the Penitents of Israel went forth out of the land of Judea and sojourned in the land of Damascus." There they joined the Essenic movement which, symbolized by the New Covenant spoken of by Prophet Jeremiah, sought to restore some measure of the righteousness of the ascetic lifestyle of the Patriarchs. The Covenant bound them to distinguish between clean and unclean, sacred and profane, to love one another as they loved themselves, and to care for the needy, the poor, and the sojourner. In accordance with the Mosaic law, they were to keep the Sabbath, the festivals, and the Day of Atonement. Nevertheless, not all of the Essenes moved to Qumran. Evidence suggests that many of these "Elect of Israel" of the Latter Days remained in the northern districts of

Palestine where they established settlements. Here they encountered other groups holding similar, but not identical, beliefs carrying on the old ascetic Nazarene way of life. The term Essean or Essene of the northern Aramaic word "chaya" and Greek "hosies" (saint) is generic in nature and applicable to a variety of loosely related groups or sects. In this sense, the Nazarenes were just a sect. They held some beliefs that were similar to the beliefs expressed in the Qumran Scrolls, and other beliefs that bear little or no similarity to some of the beliefs and practices mentioned in the Scrolls. From a religious perspective, the reason for this is obvious: the beliefs of the Nazarenes were derived from Jesus' teachings, which for the most part were based upon divine revelations received by him from God. It was these revelations that formed Jesus' Gospel in the technical sense.

The Gospel of Barnabas and the Qumran Scrolls

On the other hand, despite the good intentions of the Essenes in general, their own literature, as distinct from other writings in their collection, is not holy writ, but rather the interpretations, rules and regulations to which they subscribed.

When we read *The Gospel of Barnabas* with the Qumran Scrolls, we find striking similarities between it and some of the beliefs expressed in the Scrolls. This fact alone forces one to say that in antiquity and authenticity, no other gospel can come close to *The Gospel of Barnabas*. If it were a forgery, as it is alleged, it would not be so rich in the Essenic terminology of Jesus' time. The Greek manuscripts are very poor in this area.

The Qumran Scrolls were not discovered until 1947; therefore, no forger prior to the discovery and translation of the Scrolls could have known Essenic terminology in such abundance when virtually nothing was known about them. *The Gospel of Barnabas* can be easily traced back through tradition and historical documentation to the Apostles Barnabas and Matthew as this work will demonstrate.

In chapter 108 of *The Gospel of Barnabas*, he relates how Jesus explained that there were many people who thought him insane because he chose to live in poverty, and not in opulence among princes. This attitude must have been commonly held by non-Essenes against those who chose to live in the manner of the Essenes. This statement alone in relation to the period in which it was spoken by Jesus, identifies him with the Essenes who led an ascetic life.

Besides, the members of the Qumran community, as we know from the *Manual of Discipline,* called themselves "the elect" or "the elect of God":

> The members of the community will be in all justice the witnesses of God's truth and the *elect of His favor*, affecting

atonement for the earth and ensuring the requital of the wicked (VIII: 1-19).

Now read the following passage from *The Gospel of Barnabas* 52:

> The judgement day of God will be so dreadful that verily, I say to you the reprobates would sooner choose ten hells than go to hear God speak in wrath against them, against whom all things created will witness. Verily, I say to you that not alone shall the reprobates fear, but the saints and *the elect of God*, so that Abraham shall not trust in his righteousness, and Job shall have no confidence in his innocence.

In the Essenic Book of Hymns, it is frequently stated that the faithful stand in the eternal congregation of God, where they hold direct conversations with Him and "share the lot of the holy beings":

> I am thankful unto Thee O Lord, for Thou hast illumined (my face) with the vision of Thy truth; wherefore I yet shall walk in everlasting glory along with all (the holy that hear the words of) Thy mouth (The Book of Hymns III, 3).

We read further in the *Manual of Discipline*:

> No member of the community — that is, no duly covenanted member — who blatantly deviates in any particular form from the total body of commandments is to be permitted to come into contact with the purity enjoyed by these specially *holy men* or to benefit by their counsel until his actions be free of all perversity, and so on (VIII: 1-19).

Now consider the presence of a similar reverential attitude for the holy ones, as expressed in *The Gospel of Barnabas*:

> Then answered he who writes, 'O master, how can we always have God in memory? Assuredly, it seems to us impossible!' Said Jesus with a sigh, 'This is the greatest misery that man can suffer, O Barnabas. For here upon earth man cannot have God his creator always in memory; *saving them that are holy, for they always have God in memory, because they have in them the light of the grace of God, so that they cannot forget God*' (*The Gospel of Barnabas* 109).

Even Jesus' statement concerning "the light of the grace of God" being in the heart of the holy ones bears striking resemblance to the attitude of the Essenes. For over and over again we find thanks being given to God in the Book of Hymns for "illuminating the face" of His servant or for shinning His light in His servant's heart.

Some Parallels Between Essene and Nazarene Beliefs

As pointed out by Prof. Gaster in his studies of the Scrolls, the Qumran community believed that even if the Torah was correctly expounded by prophet and teacher, men can receive it only if they are correctly attuned, and that this attunement comes through inner "enlightnment." The Essenes considered themselves not only the righteous remnant of Israel but also the specially "enlightened." Consequently, over and over again in the Book of Hymns, the Qumran community gives thanks to God for "illuminating the face" of His servant or for shining His light in His servant's heart. The acquisition of this light is attributed to the voluntary exercise of that power of discernment which God placed in every creature at the moment of its creation.[4] The Nazarene parallel to this belief is found in chapter seventy-eight of *The Gospel of Barnabas,* where Jesus says:

> Verily, I say to you that our God in creating man not only created him righteous, but inserted in his heart a light that should show him what is fitting to serve God. Therefore, even if this light be darkened after sin, it is not extinguished, for every nation has this desire to serve God, though they have God and serve false and lying gods.

"The typical Jewish expectation," says Dr. Davies, "had been concerned with all Israel and its characteristic context was terrestrial; the Essenes, however, to quote Josephus, 'in agreement with the opinions of the Greeks, declare that there lies away across the ocean a habitation for the good souls.'"[5] This Essenic concept of a terrestrial paradise spoken of by Josephus and a number of Greek writers, is also paralleled in *The Gospel of Barnabas* in which Jesus goes on to say in chapter seventy-eight about enlightenment:

> Accordingly, it is necessary that a man be taught of the

---

[4]Trans. Theodor H. Gaster, *The Dead Sea Scriptures,* Anchor Books, Doubleday & Co., Inc., Garden City, N.Y., 1964, pp. 66.

[5]A. Powell Davies, *The Meaning of the Dead Sea Scrolls,* The New American Library of World Literature Inc., New York, 1961, p. 66.

prophets of God, for they have clear light to teach the way to go *to paradise, our country,* by serving God well: just as it is necessary that he who has his eyes diseased should be guided and helped.

This concept of an earthly paradise is tied in with the concept that heaven and hell begins in this life, particularly in the case of Jesus' Gospel, for he also spoke of the celestial paradise.

Now whereas the Jews seem to have prayed three times a day as stated in Psalms 55:17, and Daniel 6:10, the *Manual of Discipline,* columns 10-11 read with *The Gospel of Barnabas* conveys the impression that the Essenes in general, like the Nazarene in particular, recognized five or six periods a day for devotion. The present evidence suggests that only the Nazarenes actually prayed five times a day. In the *Manual of Discipline* we find:

(Day and night I offer my praise)
and at all the appointed times which God has prescribed.
When daylight begins its rule .... (dawn)
When it reaches its turning-point .... (midday)
and when it again withdraws to its appointed abode .. (sunset, or first-star)
When the watches of darkness begin .... (evening)
when God opens the storehouse thereof
when He sets that darkness against the light .... (night)
when it reaches its turning point .... (midnight)
and when it again withdraws in face of light" .... (dawn of next day)

In the gospel history compiled by Matthew and Barnabas, we find that these hours are mentioned at various places in the text as time of prayer, and that Jesus and his apostles observed them:

Then said John, 'Teach us, for love of God, of the faith.'
Jesus answered, 'It is time that we say the *prayer of the dawn.*'
Whereupon they arose, and having washed themselves made prayer to our God, who is blessed forevermore (*The Gospel of Barnabas* 89).

When he had made the *midday prayer,* Jesus, as he went out of the temple, found one blind from his mother's womb (*The Gospel* 146).

Then said Jesus, 'Let us for three days make prayer and fast, and from henceforth *every evening when the first star shall appear, when prayer is made to God,* let us make prayer three times, asking Him three times for mercy: because the sin of

Israel is three times more grievous than other sins' (*The Gospel of Barnabas* 100).

Jesus answered, 'The hour of prayer draws near; therefore, when *the evening prayer* is ended I will tell you the meaning of the parables' (*The Gospel of Barnabas* 133).

His disciples drew near to Jesus after *the nightly prayer* and said, 'O Master, what must we do to escape pride?' (*The Gospel of Barnabas* 131).

After *the prayer of midnight* the disciples came near to Jesus (*The Gospel of Barnabas* 82).

Even the account of Jesus' birth, as related by the Apostle Barnabas, implies an affiliation of the Nazarenes with the Essenic movement. Jesus is referred to as a "holy one of God," an Essenic term applicable to one who is Essene. The opening statement of the account of his birth, *"In these last years,"* is Essenic in nature, because the Essenes were also known as the "Elect of Israel of the *Latter Days*." The Essenes held the belief that they were in the last days, or last years before the great battle was to take place between the "Sons of Light" and the "Sons of Darkness," followed by the beginning of a "new age."

In *these last years* a virgin called Mary of the lineage of David, of the tribe of Judah, was visited by the angel Gabriel from God. This virgin, living in all holiness without any offence, being blameless, and abiding in prayer with fasting, being one day alone, there entered into her chamber the angel Gabriel, and he saluted her, saying, 'God be with you O Mary.' The virgin was frightened at the appearance of the angel; but the angel comforted her saying, 'Fear not, for you have found favor with God, who has chosen you to be mother of a prophet, whom He will send to the people of Israel in order that they may walk in his laws with truth of heart.' The virgin answered, 'Now how shall I bring forth sons, seeing that I know not a man?' The angel answered, 'O Mary, God who made man without a man is able to generate in you man without a man, because with Him nothing is impossible.' Mary answered, 'I know that God is Almighty, therefore His will be done.' The angel said, 'Now be conceived in you the prophet whom you shall name Jesus, and you shall keep him from wine and from strong drink and from every unclean meat, because the child is a holy one of God.' Mary bowed herself with humility, saying, 'Behold the handmaid of God, be it done according to the word.' The angel departed, and the virgin glorified God saying, 'Know, O my soul, the greatness of God, and exult my spirit, in God my Savior, for He has regarded the lowliness of His handmaiden, in so much that I shall be called blessed by all the nations, for He that is mighty has made me great, and blessed be His holy name. For his mercy extends from generation to generation of them that fear him. Mighty has He made His hand, and He has scattered the proud in the imagination of His heart. He has put down the mighty from their seat, and has exalted the humble. Him who has been hungry has He filled with food things, and the rich He has sent away. For He keeps in memory the promises made to Abraham and to His son forever (*The Gospel of Barnabas* 1).

The divine command: "...you shall keep him from wine and from strong drink and from every unclean meat," is in accordance with the "old Arabian lifestyle" of the Patriarchs and prophets. As such, it was undeniably a divine order to Mary. As pointed out by William Smith about the Rechabites and their struggle to stay faithful to the Abrahamic Covenant with God: "The luxury and license of Phoenician cities threatened the destruction of the simplicity of their nomadic life (Amos II. 7, 8, VI. 3-6). A protest was needed against both evils, and as in the case of Elijah and of the Nazarites of Amos II, 11, it took the form of asceticism. There was to be a more rigid adherence than ever to the old Arab life."[6] The same was now true of Hellenism, the luxury and license of which had already destroyed the moral fiber of the Israelite children of Abraham, and was probably affecting Ishmaelites who had thus far resisted it. The new affirmation of the Abrahamic Covenant by the inhabitants of Palestine collectively referred to Hasidim, or Essene, is also reflected in the preceding divine command concerning Jesus and the manner in which he was to live. This new affirmation of the Abrahamic Covenant by the Essenic movement was fully in line with the prevailing view that the eternal Covenant was to be periodically reaffirmed, and that the one concluded at Sinai, (the Torah), was a rearticulation of the sacred pact that God had made with Abraham.

Thematic Coherence between
The Gospel of Barnabas and Genuine Scholarship

The inalterable nature of the essential aspect of the divinely inspired

---

[6]William Smith, *Smith's Bible Dictionary,* Article: Rechab and Levites, Pyramid Publications, New York, 1974, pp. 565-566.

Abrahamic religion is expressed by Jesus in *The Gospel of Barnabas:*

> Then asked Andrew, 'Now how shall the truth be known?'
> Jesus answered, 'Everything that conforms to the book of Moses, that you receive is true; seeing that God is one, the truth is one; whence it follows that the doctrine is one and the meaning of the doctrine is one; and therefore the faith is one' (*The Gospel of Barnabas* 124).

A number of Christian scholars once believed that Jesus was raised in accordance with the religious practices of the Jews living in southern Palestine during the second century AD. *The Gospel of Barnabas*, however, informs us that this Jewish milieu was a corrupted form of the Abrahamic religion. It was also erroneously believed at the time that this corrupted religion was prevalent throughout much of Palestine. As a result of their study of rabbinical literature, many such scholars now realize that the inhabitants of northern and southern Palestine differed on many issues. It has also come to light that the Galileans had remained more faithful to the Abrahamic religion than their southern kinsmen, despite the efforts of the southerners to destroy its purer form.[7]

Time and again *The Gospel of Barnabas* reminds its readers that the birth of Jesus was not the advent of a new religion, but to preserve the purity of the Abrahamic faith. This is self-evident from the following statement — a mangled version of which is found in the Hellenized manuscript erroneously attributed to Matthew by the Gentiles:

> Jesus said, 'You think that I am come to destroy the law and the prophets? Verily I say to you, as God lives, I have not come to destroy it, but rather to observe it. For every prophet has observed the law of God and all that God by the other prophets has spoken. As God lives, in whose presence my soul stands, no one who breaks the least precept can be pleasing to God, but shall be least in the kingdom of God, for he shall have no part there. Moreover I say to you that one syllable of the law of God cannot be broken without the gravest sin. But I want you to know that it is necessary to observe that which God said by Isaiah the prophet with these words, 'Wash you and be clean, take away your thoughts from mine eyes.

---

[7] Hugh J. Schonfield, *The Passover Plot*, Bantam Books, New York, 1969, p. 31.

'Verily, I say to you that all the water of the sea will not wash him who with his heart loves iniquities' (*The Gospel of Barnabas* 38).

The Nazarenes, like the Essenes in general, did not seek to establish a new religion: they sought a reaffirmation of the Abrahamic Covenant.

The Essenes, as scholarly research demonstrates, were correct in their stance that long before the rise of the newly named Christianity the Scriptures of the Jews had been tampered with.[8] In chapter sixty-eight, as well as elsewhere in *The Gospel of Barnabas*, one finds this same Essenic argument. Jesus is reported to have said in his answer to a question by a high priest:

You ask me to tell you what God will give us in paradise. Verily, I say to you that those who think of the wages love not the master. A shepherd who has a flock of sheep, when he sees the wolf coming, prepares to defend them; while the hireling, when he sees the wolf leaves the sheep and flees. As God lives, in whose presence I stand, if the God of our fathers were your God you would not have thought of saying, 'What will God give me?' But you would have said as did David his prophet, 'What shall I give to God for all that he has given to me?'

I will speak to you by a parable that you may understand. There was a king who found by the wayside a man stripped by thieves, who had wounded him to death. He had compassion on him, and commanded his slaves to bear that man to the city and tend him; and this they did with all diligence. The king conceived a great love for the sick man so much so that he gave him his own daughter in marriage and made him his heir. Now assuredly this king was most merciful; but the man beat the slaves, despised the medicines, abused his wife, spoke evil of the king, and caused his vassals to rebel against him. When the king required any service, he would as usual say, 'What will the king give me as reward?' Now when the king heard this, what did he do to so impious a man?

They all replied, 'Woe to him, for the king deprived him of all, and sternly punished him.' Then said Jesus, 'O Priests and Scribes and Pharisees, and you high-priest that hear my voice, I

---

[8]Theodor H. Gaster, op. cit., pp 5-6.

proclaim to you what God has said to you by his prophet Isaiah: 'I have nourished slaves and exalted them, but they have despised Me.'

The king is our God, who found Israel in a world full of miseries, and gave him therefore to his servants Joseph, Moses and Aaron, who tended him. And our God conceived such love for him that for the sake of the people of Israel He struck Egypt, drowned Pharaoh, and discomfited an hundred and twenty kings of the Canaanites and Madianites. He gave him His laws, making him heir of all that land wherein our people dwell.

But how does Israel bear himself? How many prophets has he slain; *how many (books of the) prophets has he contaminated; how has he violated the law of God: how many for that cause have departed from God to serve idols, through your offence, O priests!* And now you ask me, 'What will God give us in paradise?' You ought to have asked me, 'What will be the punishment that God will give you in hell and then what you ought to do for true penitence in order that God may have mercy on you: for this I can tell you, and to this end am I sent to you' (*The Gospel of Barnabas* 68).

Jesus' Charge of Corruption Against the Jews

A more definite reference to the corruption of the Scriptures by the impious among the Jews is found in chapter 124 of *The Gospel of Barnabas* in response to a question by James:

> James inquired, 'O Master, if perchance there shall come a false prophet and lying teacher pretending to instruct us, what should we do?'
>
> Jesus answered in parable, 'A man goes to fish with a net, and therein he catches many fish, but those that are bad he throws away.
>
> A man went forth to sow, but only the grain that falls on good ground bears seed.
>
> Even so should you do, listening to all and receiving only the truth, seeing that the truth alone bear fruit to eternal life.'
>
> Then asked Andrew, 'Now how shall the truth be known?'
>
> Jesus answered, '*Everything that you receive is true if it conforms to the book of Moses: seeing that God is one, the truth is one. As such, it follows that the doctrine is one and the meaning of the doctrine is one. Verily, I say to you that if the truth had not been erased from the book of Moses, God would*

not have given to David our father the second. And if the book of David had not been contaminated, God would not have committed the Gospel to me. See that the Lord our God is unchangeable and has spoken but one message to all men'
(*The Gospel of Barnabas* 123-124).

Research by a number of scholars has yielded the same charges of corruption against the Jews.

During the 6th century BC, there came about a period in which many psalms falsely attributed to David were written. The second half of the book of Isaiah was also written at this time and falsely attributed to the Prophet Isaiah. During another episode of such activity, the Torah (Genesis, Exodus, Leviticus, Numbers, Deuteronomy) was rewritten, and insertions and omissions were made along with a number of glosses. Additional psalms were written and again falsely attributed to David, while the Song of Songs (Song of Solomon) attributed to Solomon was actually written during this time and therefore could not have been of Solomon's authorship, though it was probably derived in part from older material dating back to him. Ruth and the present form of Jonah were also produced during this period. Indeed, as the Essenes and Jesus have correctly said, the Jews have corrupted the Scripture and added manuscripts to it in the name of divine revelation. In addition to the preceding works and corruptions of the Scripture, there are I and II Chronicles — a rewritten version of Samuel and Kings — in which much of the older material was omitted to produce one favorable to the priesthood by diminishing the role of the monarch. Ecclesiastes and the present form of Proverbs and Job are all the rewritten handiwork of the impious. And all of this, it must be remembered, was done before the advent of Jesus the Messiah who clearly stated that Jewish impiety is the reason he was sent to them by God. It is these corrupted and spurious books that the Gentiles unscrupulously incorporated into their book *The Bible.*[9]

Jesus' Birth — The Reaffirmation of the Abrahamic Faith

The birth of Jesus is such an important event in the revival of Abrahamic faith that even Joseph is cautioned by the angel to ensure that Jesus is brought up in the old Abrabian way:

---

[9]Samuel Sandmel, *Judaism and Christian Beginnings,* Oxford University Press, New York, 1978, pp. 21-23.
See also John Lewis, *The Religions of the World Made Simple,* Made simple Books, Inc., New York, 1958, p. 77.

Mary having known the will of God, fearing the people, lest they should take offense at her being pregnant with child, and should stone her as guilty of fornication, chose a companion of her own lineage, a man by name called Joseph, of blameless life: for he as a righteous man feared God and served Him with fasting and prayer, living by the work of his hands, for he was a carpenter.

Such a man the virgin knowing, chose him for her companion and revealed to him the divine counsel.

Joseph, being a righteous man, was thinking about putting Mary away when he perceived that she was pregnant with child because he feared God. Behold, while he slept, he was rebuked by the angel of God, saying, 'O Joseph, why do you want to put away Mary your wife? Know that whatever she has been carrying in her has all been done by the will of God. The virgin shall bring forth a son, whom you shall call Jesus; *whom you shall keep away from wine and from strong drink and every unclean meat,* because he is a holy one of God from his mother's womb. He is a prophet of God sent to the people of Israel so that he may convert Judah to his heart, and that Israel may walk in the law of the Lord, as it is written in the law of Moses. He shall come with great power, which God shall give him, and shall work great miracles, whereby many shall be saved.'

Joseph, arising from sleep, gave thanks to God, and lived with Mary all his life, serving God with all sincerity (*The Gospel of Barnabas* 2).

The theme of the spiritual superiority of the "old Arab life" of the Patriarchs is further alluded to when, in accordance with the divine will of God, the first shelter that Jesus had from the weather was a shepherd's cottage. The shepherd's occupation symbolizes the purity of the old Arab life which, as expressed by the Abrahamic religion, is by one's shelter against the harm of this world:

> There reigned at that time in Judea Herod, by decree of Caesar Augustus, and Pilate was governor in the priesthood of Annas and Caiaphas. By decree of Augustus, all the world was enrolled so everybody went to his own country and they presented themselves by their own tribes to be enrolled. Joseph accordingly departed from Nazareth, a city of Galilee, with Mary his wife, pregnant with child, to go to Bethlehem (for that it was his city, he being of the lineage of David) in order that he

might be enrolled according to the decree of Caesar. Joseph having arrived at Bethlehem, for that city was small, and great was the multitude of them who were strangers there, found no place. Thus, he took lodging outside the city in *a shepherd's shelter*. While Joseph lived there, the days were fulfilled for Mary to bring forth. The virgin was surrounded by a light exceedingly bright, and brought forth her son without pain, whom she took in her arms and wrapping him in swaddling-clothes, laid him in the manger, because there was no room in the inn. There came with gladness a great multitude of angels to the inn, blessing God and announcing peace to them who fear God. Mary and Joseph praised the Lord for the birth of Jesus, and with greatest joy nurtured him (*The Gospel of Barnabas* 3).

And again, the theme is continued in the life of Jesus. Shepherds living the ascetic life of the Patriarchs and prophets rather than the city dwellers are summoned first by the angel of God to see and greet the new born babe, who himself was to be raised in line with the "old Arab lifestyle:"

At that time *the shepherds* were watching over their flock, as is their custom. And behold, they were surrounded by an exceedingly bright light, out of which apeared to them an angel, who blessed God. The shepherds were filled with fear by reason of the sudden light and the appearance of the angel. 'Behold, I announce to you a great joy, for there is born in the city of David a child who is a prophet of the Lord; who brings great salvation to the house of Israel. The child you shall find in the manger, with his mother, who blesses God.' And when he had said this there came a great multitude of angels blessing God, announcing peace to them that have good will. After the angels had departed, the shepherds spoke among themselves, saying: 'Let us go to Bethlehem and see the word which God by his angel has announced to us.' There came many shepherds to Bethlehem seeking the newborn babe, and they found outside the city the child who was born, according to the word of the angel, lying in the manger. They therefore made obeisance to him, and gave to the mother that which they had, announcing to her what they had heard and seen. Mary therefore kept all these things in her heart, and Joseph likewise, giving thanks to God. The shepherds returned to their flock, announcing to everyone how great a thing they had seen. And so the whole hill country of Judea was filled with fear, and every man laid up this word in his heart, saying: 'What, think we, shall this child be?' (*The Gospel of Barnabas* 4).

Obedience to the Abrahamic Covenant and its reaffirmation on Mount Sinai is demonstrated in the simple act of obeying the will of God expressed in the Law:

> When the eight days were fulfilled *according to the law of the Lord, as it is written in the book of Moses, they took the child and carried him to the temple to circumcise him.* And so they circumcised the child and gave him the name Jesus, as the angel of the Lord had said before he was conceived in the womb. Mary and Joseph perceived that the child was for the salvation and ruin of many. Therefore, they feared God, and kept the child with fear of God (*The Gospel of Barnabas* 5).

In that portion of the account involving the magi (wise men), it is not said from which land in the east they had come to see the new born babe. The term "magi," though indicative of Persian wisemen, is nevertheless inconclusive in identifying the area east of Palestine, since it was also used for men of wisdom, spiritual or temporal. Two things are known, though not conclusive. First, that they were from the "east," a term indicative of Arabia. This is plausible because of the cultural roots of Israel in Arabia. Second, Arabia was looked upon as a place in which wise men were also to be found (Jeremiah 49:7; and I Kings 4:30).

> In the reign of Herod, king of Judea when Jesus was born, three magi in the parts of *the east* were observing the stars. A star of great brightness appeared to them and, after discussing the matter they followed the star to Judea. Having arrived at Jerusalem, they asked where was born the King of the Jews. When Herod heard this, he was frightened and all the city was troubled. Herod called the priests and the scribes, saying, 'Where will the Messiah be born?' They answered that he should be born in Bethlehem; for thus it is written by the prophet: 'And thou, Bethlehem, art not little among the princes of Judah: for out of thee shall come forth a leader, who shall lead my people Israel.'
> Herod accordingly called together the magi and asked them about their coming. They answered that they had seen a star in *the east*, which had guided them to this place and wished to pay

homage with gifts to this new King manifested by his star.

Then said Herod, 'Go to Bethlehem and search for the child with all diligence, and when you have found him, come and tell me, because I would like to come and pay homage to him.' And this he spoke deceitfully.

The magi therefore left Jerusalem, and lo, the star which appeared to them in the east went before them. Seeing the star the magi were filled with gladness. And so having come to Bethlehem, outside the city, they saw the star standing still above the inn where Jesus was born. The magi went there and entering the dwelling found the child with his mother. Bending down, they did obesiance to him. The magi presented to him spices, with silver and gold, recounting to the virgin all that they had seen.

While sleeping, they were warned by the child not to go to Herod. So departing by another way, they returned to their own home, announcing all they had seen in Judea.

Herod, seeing that the magi did not return, believed that they had mocked him. He therefore decided to kill the child. But while Joseph was sleeping, there appeared to him the angel of the Lord, saying:

'Arise up quickly, and take the child with his mother and *go into Egypt*, for Herod wills to slay him.' Joseph arose with great fear, and took Mary with the child, and *they went into Egypt*, and there they lived until the death of Herod. In the meantime Herod believing himself derided by the magi, sent his soldiers to slay all the new-born children in Bethlehem. The soldiers therefore came and slew all the children that were there, as Herod had commanded them. Thus the words of the prophets were fulfilled, saying: 'Lamentation and great weeping are there in Ramah; Rachel lamented for her sons, but consolation is not given her because they are not.

When Herod was dead, the angel of the Lord appeared in a dream to Joseph, saying: 'Return into Judea, for they are dead that willed the death of the child.' Joseph therefore took the child (who was now seven years old) with Mary and came to Judea. Hearing that Archelaus, son of Herod, was reining in Judea, he went into Galilee. Fearing to remain in Judea, they went to dwell at Nazareth.

The child grew in grace and wisdom before men.

Jesus, having reached the age of twelve years, went up with Mary and Joseph *to worship there according to the law of the*

Lord written in the book of Moses. When their prayers were ended they departed, having lost Jesus, because they thought he had returned home with their kinsfolk. Mary therefore returned with Joseph to Jerusalem seeking Jesus among kinsfolk and neighbors. On the third day they found the child in the temple, in the midst of the doctors, disputing with them concerning the law. And everyone was amazed at his questions and answers, saying, 'How can there be such doctrine in him, seeing he is so small and has not yet learned to read?'

Mary reproved him saying, 'Son, what have you done to us? I and your father have sought you for three days sorrowing.' Jesus answered, 'Don't you know that the service of God comes before father and mother?' Jesus then went down to Nazareth, and was subject to them with humility and reverence (*The Gospel of Barnabas* 6-9).

THE DUSK, THE BEGINNING OF THE AGE OF THE GENTILES

Two ongoing series of historical events led to the coming of Jesus and the predominantly Gentile representation of him as a deity. In this chapter we will first consider those events; next, we will consider in part the other series of events which contributed to creating the cultural climate in which men like Julius Caesar, Augustus Caesar, and Jesus the Nazarene would be looked upon as god.

The Waywardness of the Israelites

Throughout the Israelite history down to the time of Jesus, God repeatedly made known His will to them through the prophets so that as a chosen people they could be an example to mankind of His mercy. But the high standard of morality required of the adherents of the Abrahamic religion was often difficult for the Israelites to live up to. Added to this, their Canaanite neighbors enticed them to lower themselves to their level of morality. Sometimes this led to the practice of cultic religions among the Israelites. The Ishmaelites were also no exception to this depravity. The deviation from the true Abrahamic religion was obviously there.

After the death of Solomon, the division of their Davidic kingdom resulted in two disspirited nations, easily overcome by the Assyrians and Babylonians. It was during this period of dual monarchies that minor prophets appeared, a phenomenon which continued until the time of Alexander of Macedonia.

The first of these divinely inspired men was Elijah, who denounced King Ahab for patronizing a form of Baal worship and killing a subject and impiously seizing the dead man's vineyard for his own use. To add to the historical drama, Elijah's successor Elisha annointed Jehu as God's agent to overthrow the impious Ahab and establish a new dynasty. Jehu was assisted in this conflict by Jehonadab the Arab and the rest of the Ishmaelites who, as co-inheritors of the promised land, were still loyal to God and His covenant with their forefather Prophet Abraham.

One might well remember that in the book of Genesis we learn from God's promise to Abraham that his seed would inherit the promised land (Genesis 17:6-8). In accordance with God's will, the Ishmaelites shared in the promised land by way of the Rechabite branch of the Arab descendants of Abraham (Numbers 10:29-33; Judges 1:16). The Rechabite Arabs and the Israelite sect known as the Nazarites were puritanical remnants of Israel's desert heritage who appear intermittently in the Bible. Relevant evidence suggests that they played a larger role in the spiritual history of Israel than previously thought, a fact long referred to by the Prophet Amos (2:11). The Rechabites as well as the Kenites and Midianites in contrast to the descendants of Keturah, represent the Ishmaelite coinheritors of the promised land as pointed out in the preceding Biblical verses. In fact, to help in the spiritual preservation of Israel, they were grafted onto the spiritually important tribe of Levi. As Levites, they contributed to the spiritual well-being of the Jewish nation, which was prone to straying from the straight path prescribed by God.[10]

The Minor Prophets

Amos was a humble herdsman. Elevated to prophethood by God, his mission was to raise God consciousness in his people and remove the anamolies in the social system of Israel. In his denounciation of the wicked, he is scornful of the religious rites which helped the rich in oppressing the poor. Amos declared the divine message to his people: "Thus says the Lord, I hate and loath your religious festivals ... when you burn offerings to me I do not enjoy your gifts, and I take no notice of your richest sacrifice." He condemned the rich because " they sell the righteous for silver and the needy for a pair of shoes, trample down the poor and squeeze load after load of corn from them." What the Lord wants is not more sacrifices but more justice. "Let judgement run down as water and righteousness as a mighty stream." Amos foretold the political and military disaster that would befall them as a chastisement for their iniquities.

Isaiah, unlike Amos, was a courtier, and he was a prophet of the southern Israeli kingdom which bore the name Judah. His ministry as a prophet of God involved fifty years of activity at court as a prophet and statesman. In his criticism of the system, he lambasted the socially-sinning soldier, governor, and official, for "the men who add house to house, who join field to field, till there is room for none but them." Politically, in the turmoil of the times, with danger on all sides of the kingdom, Isaiah advocated no alliances, but advised his people to trust God. Like Amos, he too records

---

[10]William Smith, Articles: Rechab and Levites, loc. cit., op. cit., 346-347.

God's impatience with the elaborate ritual of the Temple introduced by the Israelites of Judah as a substitute for justice. As Prof. Hitti points out: "His (God's) abode was (symbolically) a tent *and his ritual was by no means elaborate.*"[11] Such was the pristine form of the Abrahamic religion among the Ishmaelites which the Israelites were corrupting with a lot of meaningless pomp and grandeur accompanied by evil ways. Isaiah warned them that God would chastise wickedness both inside and outside Israel. Here a note was struck, and it outraged the religious sentiment of a people who erroneously believed that their having been chosen by God placed them above the universal law of cause and effect. In their ignorance they questioned: How was it possible that the Lord God should punish His own people?

Throughout this time, the fertility cults so characteristic of paganism went on side by side with the worship of God among the inhabitants of both Israelite kingdoms. Their corruption of the Abrahamic religion is reflected in their tendency to worship God with rites similar to Baal worship. As a result, faithful Israelites rose against paganism, which led to the great sixth-century BC reformation under King Josiah. All local shrines were abolished and the worship of God was centralized in the Temple at Jerusalem. To protect the poor and defenseless from the tyranny of wayward kings, a number of new social and political regulations were adopted. But so stubborn were the wicked Israelites that the reformation proved ineffective. The priests were too often disposed to play up the ceremonial side of worship to the neglect of the moral requirements.

Prophet Jeremiah would have none of this and zealously condemned their pretense at reformation. The new Deuteronomic Law, a corruption of the original, became a fetish and its possession a substitute for inward submission to God.

The divine message given to Jeremiah was appalling, first to Jeremiah as a well-wisher of his people, and second to the people themselves. As one authority points out, Jeremiah realized that no Deuteronomic Law, however exalted, sane and persuasive could ever reach the stubborn heart of his people. He further realized that Temple worship had given them a completely groundless sense of self-satisfaction because of their misconception that what they were doing was correct. Without mincing words, Jeremiah told them that Yahweh (Jehovah) would totally reject them, and that the temple, believed to be inviolable, would be destroyed, since they had made it a symbol of false religion.

Jeremiah's warning was based on the divine law of cause and effect. The

---

[11]Philip K. Hitti, *History of the Arabs,* The Macmillan Co., New York, 1951, p. 40.

Israelites, however, paid no attention to Jeremiah's call. Except for a few righteous souls, others continued in their wicked way. It was with this small group of enlightened souls that the reaffirmation of the Covenant was made. The Essenes identify with this remnant in their writings. By the same token, their way of life was influenced by the ascetic way of life maintained by the Rechabites.

As God had warned the Israelites through Prophet Jeremiah, so it came to pass. In 587 BC, Jerusalem fell and the first exiles left the city. In 586 BC, following an ineffective revolt, the temple and the city were destroyed and the rest of the inhabitants were sent into captivity.

Still the majority had not learned their lesson. On two separate occasions following the exile, one of which we shall discuss here, the Israelites continued to corrupt their faith. Additions and changes were made to the Scriptures during the same time when the book of Ezekiel was compiled. Many spurious psalms were falsely attributed to David, and a fictitious document was incorporated into the book of Isaiah. Evidently, the second half of that book, as it exists today, is spurious. The only authentic Scripture produced during this period, though not necessarily in its present form, was the book of Ezekiel. The preceding theme, that their waywardness was leading them to a termination of their dispensation as a people, is also found in the book of Ezekiel. The Jews, as they began to be called at this time, were issued a warning by God that they were not going to be saved *en masse* simply because they were of the children of Abraham; but rather, they would be saved individually by their repentance. Such was God's mercy even while many of them were involved in corrupting the Scriptures and other evil deeds.

Jesus' True Mission

It was in part their corruption of the Scriptures that set the stage for Jesus' advent as the Israelite Messiah. His mission was to gather the righteous remnant of Israel and announce the termination of their dispensation as a people. As discussed already, Jesus is reported to have said in *The Gospel of Barnabas* that the corruption of the Scriptures by the Israelites was the cause of his coming. The Hellenic gospels of the New Testament do not bring out this important point. Rather, Jesus' coming is misrepresented as a bloody human sacrifice to appease God for the sins of mankind, an idea totally in accord with paganism, but in total contradiction to the divinely accepted animal sacrifices of the early stage of the Abrahamic religion (Deuteronomy 12:29-31). To identify Jesus with the burnt offerings of animal flesh is a feeble attempt by the early Gentile Church to justify paganism as the legitimate successor to the Abrahamic religion. One may read Matthew 16:21, John 1:29, Hebrews 10:1-18, Luke

22-20, and Romans 3:23-25, in that order, to see how they have presented this pagan concept of human sacrifice as a basic principle of their belief system.

However, as said before, it was not the Abrahamic religion but the Israelite dispensation that was to be replaced. In other words, the practice of the Abrahamic religion would now become more universal in nature, for its foundation is the Abrahamic Covenant with God to worship Him and Him alone as the Eternal, Indivisible Divine Being who is merciful and compassionate toward His creation. The divine law would change only in the sense of becoming more universal in its relationship toward all of mankind's proper needs.

Common sense and divine revelation dictate that the dispensation predestined to succeed the Israelite dispensation could not be based upon paganism. Jesus was no preacher of adherence to blind faith. We read in *The Gospel of Barnabas*:

> When it was early Friday morning, Jesus assembled his disciples after the prayer and said to them, 'Let us sit down, for as on this day God created man of the clay of the earth, so will I tell you what a thing is man, if God pleases.'
>
> When all were seated, Jesus said again, 'Our God, to show to His creatures His goodness and mercy and His omnipotence, with His liberality and justice, made a composition of four things contrary one to the other, and united them in one final object, which is man — and this is earth, air, water, and fire — in order that each one might temper its opposite. He made of these four things a vessel, which is man's body, of flesh, bones, blood, marrow, and skin, with nerves and veins, and with all his inward parts; wherein God placed the soul and the senses, as two hands of this life: lodging a sense in every part of the body, for it diffused itself there like oil. And to the soul He gave the heart, where, united with the senses, it should rule the whole life.
>
> God, having thus created man, put into him a light called reason, which was to unite the flesh, the senses, and the soul in a single end — to work for the service of God.
>
> After this, He placed this work in paradise. However, as reason was seduced through the sense by Satan, the flesh lost its rest, the senses lost the delight whereby they live, and the soul lost its beauty.
>
> Man having come to such a plight, the senses, which find not repose in labor, but seeks delight, not being curbed by reason,

follow the light which the eyes show them. The eyes not being able to see anything but vanity, deceive themselves, and so, choosing earthly things, sins.

Thus it is necessary that by the mercy of God, man's reason be enlightened afresh to know good from evil, and (to distinguish) the true delight, knowing which the sinner is converted to penitence. Therefore, I say to you that if God our Lord enlightens not the heart of man, the reasoning of men are of no avail.'

John asked, 'Then to what end serves the speech of men?'

Jesus replied, 'Man as man cannot convert man to penitence, but man used by God converts man. Since God works by a secret fashion in man's salvation, one should listen to every man so that among all may be received Him in whom God speaks to us.'

James asked, 'O Master, if perchance there shall come a false prophet and lying teacher pretending to instruct us, what should we do?'

Jesus answered in parable, 'A man goes to fish with a net, and therein he catches many fish, but those that are bad he throws away.

A man went forth to sow, but only the grain that falls on good ground bears seed.

Even so ought you to do, listening to all and receiving only the truth, seeing that the truth bears fruit unto eternal life.'

Then asked Andrew, 'Now how shall the truth be known?'

Jesus answered, 'Everything that you receive that conforms to the book of Moses is true; seeing that God is one, the truth is one; whence it follows that the doctrine is one and the meaning of the doctrine is one; and therefore the faith is one. *Verily, I say to you that if the truth had not been erased from the book of Moses, God would not have given to David our father the second. And if the book of David had not been contaminated, God would not have committed the Gospel to me; seeing that the Lord our God is unchangeable, and has spoken but one message to all men. As such, when the messenger of God shall come, he shall come to cleanse away all wherewith the ungodly have contaminated my book*' (*The Gospel of Barnabas 123-124*).

Jesus' prophesy of the messenger of God to come is in line with the essential aspect of Essene thought. The Essenes looked forward to the coming of the prophet who would usher in a new age in which "the earth would be filled with the knowledge of the Lord God like the waters which cover the sea."[12] The belief in the prophet who was to come is based upon Moses' prophecy *(Deuteronomy* 18:15-19). Jesus nor his true followers the Nazarenes looked upon him as being "that prophet." Rather, like other teachers of the Essenic movement, he foretold his coming. But while Jesus as a prophet of God may be expected to be accurate in his prophecies, we should allow for discrepancies in the predictions of other Essenic teachers concerning that Prophet. More will be said of this later.

The Coming of the Gentiles

At this point, let us consider some of the events leading up to the establishment of a cultural climate in which men such as Julius Caesar and Jesus were declared gods.

To the Semitic people, both Ishmaelite and Israelite, a series of warnings concerning the Gentiles, and "the age of the Gentiles," were given, which is now probably approaching its end. It was prophesied that the Gentiles would dominate the earth for the time alloted to them as others had done before them. The Israelites were given the warning first, before the time of Jesus the Messiah, and the Ishmaelites were given the warning after the time of Jesus

According to the religious tradition of the Israelites, which are also found among the present-day Jews, an Israelite is one who is either born of an Israelite mother or has converted to the Israelite expression of the Abrahamic religion; all others are known by them as goyim ("non-Jewish"). In their doctrines, the goyim (Gentiles) are divided into groups: pagans and monotheists. The latter worship the true God, who stands alone, indivisible, without equals, relatives or partners. These non-pagans are abiding by the seven Nochian Laws, which according to the Talmud — a book of the Jews — is derived from the early chapters of Genesis, prohibiting injustice, blasphemy, idolatry, sexual immorality, murder, robbery and eating part of a live animal.[13]

In the King James version of the Bible, the term Gentile (goyim) is openly applied to the descendants of Noah's son Japheth in the tenth chapter of the book of Genesis, while the warnings to the Israelites concerning the Gentiles is to be found in Deuteronomy 28:25; Jeremiah 1:11-16; Zechariah 1:18-21; and Daniel 7:1-7. Warnings to the Ishmaelites concerning the Gentiles is contained in the Qur'an, specifically the 18th

---

[12]Theodor H. Gaster, op. cit., p. 6.
[13]Ben Isaacson, *Dictionary of the Jewish Religion,* Article: Gentile, Bantam Books Inc., New York, 1979, p. 206.

28 *The Dusk, the beginning of the age of the Gentiles*

surah, and in the Hadith. To go into detail here would be digressing from the main theme of this work.

In the composite work known as the book of Daniel, which utilizes a variety of sources including perhaps the original Book of Daniel, chapter two alludes to the advent of the age of Gentiles. King Nebuchadnezzar had the first dream concerning the age of the Gentiles, and Daniel is interpreting it for him.

> This is the dream, and we will tell its interpretation before the king. Thou, O king, art a king of kings; for the God of heaven has given thee a kingdom, power, and strength, and glory.
>
> And wherever the children of men dwell, the beasts of the field and the fowls of the heaven has He given into thine hand, and hath made thee ruler over them all. Thou art this head of gold.
>
> And after you shall arise another kingdom inferior to yours, and another third kingdom of bronze, which shall bear rule over all the earth.
>
> And the fourth kingdom shall be strong as iron, forasmuch as iron breaks in pieces and subdues all things; and as iron that breaks all these, shall it break in pieces and bruise.
>
> And whereas you saw the feet and toes, part of potter's clay and part of iron, the kingdom shall be divided; but there shall be in it of the strength of the iron, for as much as you saw the iron mixed with miry clay.
>
> And as the toes of the feet were part of iron and part of clay, so the kingdom shall be partly strong and partly broken.
>
> And whereas you saw iron mixed with miry clay, they shall mingle themselves with the seed of men; but they shall not adhere one to another; even as iron is not mixed with clay (Daniel 2:37-43).

In the 1967 edition of the New Scofield Reference Edition of the King James Version, the four metals which made up the image in Nebuchadnezzar's dream are said to symbolize four empires: first, the Babylonian Empire (not comprised of the children of Japheth), followed by the Medo-Persian Empire (comprised primarily of Japhethinians), which began its rise with Cyaxares (625-593 BC), the founder of the Median dynasty. He first allied himself with his Scythian brethren and latter with the Babylonians through the marriage of a daughter to Nebuchadnezzar. Thus strenghtened, he attacked the Assyrians and brought their power to an end. After seventy-five years, the Median Empire was absorbed by the Persians when Astyages, who succeeded Cyaxares was deposed as king of the Median Empire by Cyrus the Great (550-530 BC). Cyrus made the Median Empire a part of Persia. He then began taking control of the Median Empire and went about conquering Lydia and Babylonia. His son, Cambyses (530-521 BC), conquered Egypt, thereby extending Persian power into Alkebu-lan (Africa).

The Third Empire

The third empire of Nebuchadnezzar's dream was that of the Greeks. Established by the Macedonians under Alexander, it was with him rather than with any of his predecessors that the "Age of the Gentiles" really began.

The expansion of Alexander's empire (356-623 BC) was eastward from Europe into Asia as far as present-day Pakistan and extended into Alkebu-lan (Africa), wresting Judea and then Egypt from Persia in the process. "In stunned silence," says Grollenberg, "the peoples of the East witnessed the meteoric rise of Alexander the Great. He appeared superhuman, this twenty-year old Macedonian who marched in victorius progress across the domains of the most venerable civilizations of the world, and in whom a supreme mastery of the art of war was coupled with a mystic's vision of world unity."[14]

But Alexander's concept of the world unity, as Grollenberg admits, involved a Hellenized (westernized) world worshipping him as its deity. He dreamed of a world empire established by his own efforts, stretching from present-day Pakistan to Gibralter and from the Danube to the source of the Nile, united by the Greek language and culture and by the worship of his supposed divine person.[15] One must bear in mind the cultural environment and education of Alexander's youth in order to understand his madness. Between Epirus and Thrace stretched the mountains, forests and grazing lands of the Macedonians. The Greek Demonsthenes considered his Macedonian kinsmen inferior to himself and the rest of the Greeks, for he looked upon the Macedonians as being little better than beasts. Of the Greeks in general, Rene Sedillot remarks: "Not only were they (the Greeks) theives but liars, braggarts and babblers as well. They were born politicians. In workshops, villages and trading-stations fierce jealousies were rife." He goes on to say: "Competition was the law of their being, and indiscipline their method. Mutual slaughter was commoner than mutual understanding. Even when peril threatened from outside they

---

[14]Grollenberg, trans. Joyce M.H.Reid, op. cit., p. 102.
[15]Ibid, p. 105

were incapable of calling a truce to their ruling passions or of uniting in self-defense."[16] Indeed, with them private interest was always of more importance than the general good, one might say they had a genuine capitalistic spirit. Greece perished because of the psychological inability of its cities to federate. Consequently, Greece is merely a geographical term. As Sedillot remarks: "The history of the ancient world was familiar only with Greek factions, divisions , and rivalries. Rome gave birth to the state. Hellas could produce only warring cities, and even within each of them individualism was rampant."[17] In general, such was the cultural background of Alexander's upbringing.

In the make-up of his mind one should not discount the influence of his parents and tutor. His father, Philip, was an ambitious man who succeeded to the Macedonian throne. The confluence of power and riches fired his passion for grandeur far beyond kingship. The Greek tendency to fabricate genealogies linking themselves with the gods was already there. Coins therefore were struck with the head of the mythical hero Hercules to spread the notion that he came from that mythical man-god. Now since in Greek beliefs the man-god Hercules was the son of the sky god Zeus, both Philip and Alexander claimed descent from these gods. This whole fabrication motivated by Greek vanity contributed to Alexander's notion of his own divinity. His mother led him to believe that he was a descendant of the Trojan hero Achilles. Finally, there was the influence of the Greek philospher Aristotle upon him, who contributed to the breadth of his scientific interests and made him reach present-day Pakistan. Again it is Aristotle who is held responsible for his love of Homeric songs and steadfast prejudice that Greek culture was superior to all others.

Alexander's successful invasion of the eastern lands truly marked the "dusk" the beginning of "The Age of the Gentiles." Success after success reinforced in his mind the notion of his own godhood, but ironically, his Greek comrades, who like many other Gentile nations were prone to worshipping man-gods, somehow could not bring themselves to worship him. He pretended to drop his claim to divinity. Nevertheless following his campaign in present-day Pakistan, he made that claim again.

Alexander's drive for world domination injected Greece into the world of international relations, but it differed from that of the Alkebulani (African) and Asian powers that had preceded it. The later established their systems of government over their empires with no thought of imposing their culture upon their conquered subjects. Some cultural

---

[16]Rene Sedillot, *The History of the World*, New American Library, New York, 1951, p. 43.
[17]Ibid.

exchanges did take place, but it was voluntary. By contrast, Alexander, a man motivated by a god-complex, and his successors desiring to carry out his dream, planted Greek colonies throughout the conquered lands.

It was not until a hundred and fifty years after his demise that the small Jewish community, isolated in the mountains of Judah far from the great coast road, felt the brutal impact of Alexander's dream of Hellenizing the eastern lands: "All men must become one people". Antiochus IV, a Greek inheritor of a portion of Alexander's empire, took up this cry and called upon the Jews inhabiting the mountains of Judah to abandon the spiritual heritage of their fathers. It was then that the Maccabees demonstrated that a living core of the old spirit of Judah still existed.

It is in the account of these troubled times that the name Alexander is first mentioned in the Scriptures. When the author of the first book of Maccabees relates the courage and successful deeds of those Jews who resisted Hellenization, he first briefly outlines its historical background. As Grollenberg points out, the Maccabean account is essentially Biblical in its outlook and choice of words when demonstrating the contrast between the transcience of Alexander's success and his claim of divine origin.[18]

The Jews reacted to this invasion in different ways. In Judea, the Jews rejected the Hellenic culture as being inferior. But outside Judia, the situation was different. Daily contacts with the Greeks were gradually Hellenizing the Jewish scene. Says Grollenberg: "There was continuous contact with the (Jewish) emigres of the Diaspora who, although they lived in their own quarters, were inevitably exposed to alien influences. Even those who had settled in Babylonia were almost as Hellenized as the Jews of Alexandria, the cultural and commercial metropolis."[19] From the same source we learn the degree of Hellenization the Jews underwent in the lands surrounding Judea as a result of the Hellenistic lifestyle that flourished in those lands. Grollenberg cites the papyri of a certain trading agent named Zeno, employed in the service of a minister of Ptolemy II Philadelphus:

> In his correspondence are several letters from an important Jew in Trans-Jordan, the governor of a 'fortress' in a crown domain which had automatically fallen to the Ptolemies. This Tobias ..., who came from the same family as the High Priest, was in continuous trading relations with Jerusalem and with merchants supplying the Egyptian court. His letters are written

---

[18]Grollenberg, trans. Joyce M. H. Reid, New York, loc. cit.
[19]Ibid., p. 105.

in *impeccable Hellenistic Greek* and does not scruple to include occasional *invocations to the gods*. We must realize that when a Jew left the territory of Judea he passed at once into Hellenistic centres where Greek was spoken, where there were Greek statues and buildings in the Greek style, theatres, gymnasia, sacred groves of the nymphs, temples, and endless colonades, and where a sound general education required that he should engage in sports and pastimes as well as in reading literature and philosophy.

As a result of this Hellenization of the Jews, elements of Greek culture, especially its philosophy, were introduced by a number of Hellenized Jews into the Abrahamic religion, which had already been corrupted by previous generations.

The Fourth Empire

Then came the Romans, the fourth beast of Daniel's vision. According to one source, the fourth Gentile power in Nebuchadnezzar's dream was the Roman Empire. The Roman power is seen as being divided, first into two (the legs), fulfilled in the division of the empire into the Eastern and Western Roman Empire, and then into ten (the toes). As a whole, the image presented in the King's dream gives the imposing outward illusion of greatness and splendor of the Gentile world power.[20]

Now whereas the dream ascribed to Nebuchadnezzar dealt only with the illusion of splendor and greatness among the Gentile nations, the visionary dream of Daniel revealed the true nature of the Gentile powers and their erroneous ideology:

> In the first year of Belshazzar, king of Babylon, Daniel had a dream and vision of his head upon his bed; then he wrote the dream and told the sum of his matters.
> Daniel spoke and said, I saw in my vision by night, and behold, the four winds of the heaven strove upon the great sea. And four beasts came up from the sea, diverse one from another.
> The first was like a lion, and he had eagle's wings; I beheld it till its wings were plucked, and it was lifted up from the earth, and made stand upon the feet as a man; and a man's heart was given to it.

---

[20] C.I. Scofield, *The New Scofield Reference Edition of the King James Version of the Bible*, Oxford University Press, Inc., New York, 1967, p.99.

And behold, another beast, a second, like to a bear, and it raised up itself on one side, and it had three ribs in the mouth of it between its teeth; and they said thus unto it, arise, devour much flesh.

After this I beheld, and Lo, another like a leopard, which had upon its back four wings of a fowl; the beast had also four heads, a dominion was given to it.

After this I saw in the night visions, and behold, a fourth beast, dreadful and terrible and exceedingly strong, and it had great iron teeth; it devoured and broke in pieces, and stamped the residue with its feet; and it was diverse from all beasts that were before it, and it had ten horns (Daniel 7:1-7).

The true nature of the Gentile powers was revealed to Daniel as rapacious and established by force. Such is the significance of the heraldic insignias of the Gentile powers as beasts or birds of prey.

In Nebuchadnezzar's dream, the fourth beast had ten toes corresponding to the ten tribes which figure in the history of the Roman people: the Illyrians, Veneti, Picentes, Messapians, Terramare, Sabines, Samnites, Latins, Umbrians, and Oscans.

The invasion of Italy by its first Gentile (Japhethinian = Indo-European) invaders took place several centuries later than that of Greece. Drawing upon the Etruscans, these invaders established the city-state of Rome. Its shepherds in some instances might have become farmers and soldiers, and its soldiers might have turned their attention to becoming lawyers, but deep in the Roman psyche there lay a heritage of fierceness and savagery. Tacitus for instance, welcomed a bloody massacre with cries of delight; Caesar had his enemies slaughtered in cold blood; Marius, in another example of Roman savagery, had the heads of the condemned brought to him while taking his meal.

The notion of human divinity, characteristic of weaker minds, despite technological achievements, manifested itself among the Romans as it had done among the Greeks and other Gentile and non-Gentile nations and tribes of the past. Like their brethren in Greece, the Romans claimed that they were descendants not only of princes, but of gods as well. This must have been at least partially due to the ancient practice of ancestor worship, which so characterizes religious beliefs of pagans.

By conquest, inheritance and dishonest diplomacy, Rome succeeded in establishing a vast empire. But the Roman expansion outward from Saterina (Italy) brought about an inward movement, especially from the eastern Mediterranean lands. Because of Alexander's conquest and colonization, the remains of the older civilizations had for centuries existed under an overlay of Hellenism. When the Romans expanded into Asia Minor, Syria, and Egypt, they encountered a lifestyle flagrant in vices, flamboyance, chicanery, individualism, and overall temperament which differed considerably from their own. The Romans were both attracted and repelled by it. As a result, Greek culture became an essential part of the curriculum studied by what became known as an educated Roman, so that a blending of Roman and Greek cultures came about in the upper echelon of Roman society. This in turn contributed to the rise of Graeco-Roman culture.

The dominance of Graeco-Roman culture led to the preservation of a cultural environment in which men — out of ignorance — could be declared gods. Furthermore, its effect upon the Jews led to their development of a syncretism, which is referred to by some as "Synagogue Judaism". The Abrahamic religion already defiled in the Scriptures now faced a new problem.

THE BEGINNING OF
THE ANTI-CHRIST DOCTRINE

The Gentile tendency to make Men Gods

By the close of the second century before the coming of Jesus, the Roman war machine had become a professional army comprised of landless men trained in violence. These men were loyal to their generals rather than to a divided Roman state. Consequently, a number of ambitious generals appeared on the Roman political scene who used their trained armies in support of the contending factions for power. The generals who came into prominence during this turbulent period of Roman history were Marius, Sulla, Pompey, and Julius Caesar.

At this point in our inquiry, we must briefly consider the accomplishments of Julius Caesar, which caused the Gentile mind to declare him a god.

Julius Caesar trained a powerful army in the course of nine years of fierce warfare against the Gentiles of Gaul (France) and Britain, and returned to Rome as the champion of the popular party. In violation of an ancient law that no legions should approach nearer the city of Rome than the little Rubicon River, Caesar marched on the city. His audacity was taken as an affront by the Senate. Thereupon, Pompey sallied forth to oppose him in the name of the Senate, but the former was no match for him. Caesar drove him from Italy, and later from Spain and Greece. He eventually defeated him at Pharsalus. The conqueror of Pompey later sailed in to make amends to the Greek cities for hardships endured by them at the hands of Pompey, and to reform the oppressive tax system. In return, the grateful Ephesians set the style for the East by proclaiming Caesar to be "a god made manifest, and the common savior of all human life."

After driving Pompey out of Egypt, he began to clear all of his enemies out of Asia Minor and Alke-bulan. With his reputation now established as a conqueror, he returned to Rome and made himself dictator for life. The senatorial party was jealous, afraid, and indignant. But Caesar went on with his enormous plans and projects: the reformation of the calendar, the rebuilding of Rome, the construction of roads, and the termination of bribery and fraud in government. He planned to conquer Germany beyond the Rhine and avenge Crassus in Persia. By now Caesar had become to all intents, the absolute dictator of the Roman Empire. And like their Greek brethren, the Roman made Caesar a god. His statue was even set up in a temple at Rome with the inscription: "To the unconquerable god." So willing were the Gentiles to make men gods.

Another man, elevated to godhood, was Augustus Caesar. He delivered to the Romans what others could not: peace, prosperity, manumission of slaves, an efficient administration free from corruption, and so on. As one scholar puts it, Augustus by today's standards successfully ran a largescale protection racket, for he exacted tributary fees for services. It did not take the Romans long to acknowledge Augustus' super human caliber. He was declared divine and praised as the unconquerable god, and revered as the "divine Savior of the World."

This Gentile attitude toward men of ability, which elevated mortals like Alexandar of Macedonia and Julius Caesar to godhood, is also seen in the case of Jesus. If the two emperors held the power of life and death over their helpless subjects, the later healed the sick and fed the poor. *The Gospel of Barnabas* talks about this tendency among the people.

> And when Jesus had said this, there was brought to him a person possessed by demons who could not speak nor see, and was deprived of hearing. Jesus, seeing their faith, raised his eyes to heaven and said, 'Lord God of our fathers, have mercy on this sick man and give him health in order that this people may know that You have sent me.'
>
> And having said this Jesus commanded the spirit to depart, saying, 'In the power of the name of God our Lord, depart, evil one, from the man.'
>
> The spirit departed and the dumb man spoke, and saw with his eyes. Every one was filled with fear, but the scribes said, 'In the power of Beelzebub, prince of the demons, he casts out the demons.'
>
> Then said Jesus, 'Every kingdom divided against itself destroys itself, and house falls upon house. If by the power of Satan, Satan be cast out, how shall his kingdom stand? And if your sons cast out Satan with the Scripture that Solomon the prophet gave them, they testify that I cast out Satan in the power of God. As God lives, blasphemy against the Holy Spirit is without remission in this and in the other world, because the wicked man of his own will reprobates himself, knowing the reprobation.'

And having said this Jesus went out of the temple. And the common people magnified him, for they brought all the sick folk whom they could gather together, and Jesus having made prayer gave to all their health. On that day in Jerusalem the Roman soldiery by the working of Satan began to stir up the common people, saying that Jesus was the God of Israel, who had come to visit his people (*The Gospel Of Barnabas 69*).

Ironically, this was said about a man who lived in a awe before the majesty of Almighty God and who called upon his people to worship one true God. *The Gospel of Barnabas* records:

> 'As God lives in whose presence I stand, you will not receive adulation from me, *but truth*. Therefore I say to you, *repent* and *turn to God* even as our fathers did after sinning, and barden not your heart.'
>
> The priests were consumed with rage at this speech, but for fear of the common people they spoke not a word.
>
> And Jesus continued saying, 'O doctors, O scribes, O Pharisees, O priests, tell me. You desire horses like calvarymen, but you desire not to go forth to war; you desire fair clothing like women, but you desire not to spin and nurture children; you desire the fruits of the field, and you desire not to cultivate the earth; you desire fish of the sea, but you desire not to go fishing; you desire honor as citizens, but you desire not the burden of the republic; and you desire tithes and firstfruits as priests, but you desire not to serve God in truth. What then shall God do with you, seeing you desire here every good without any evil? Verily, I say to you that God will give you a place where you will have every evil without any good' (*The Gospel of Barnabas 69*).

The Hellenization of a large segment of the Jews was the primary cause of their ignorance, which helped spread misconceptions concerning Jesus and his relationship to God. Following the cultures of the Gentiles, the ignorant among them developed the god-complex and, as a consequence, forgot the absolute indivisible nature of God that distingushes Him from the typical pagan deity.

Jesus Warning that the Gentiles would make Him a God

Jesus, as a messenger of God, was aware of the Gentile mind and its god-complex. He was deeply worried about its excesses. In a passage

38 The Beginning of the anti-Christ Doctrine

unsurpassed in its monotheistic theme and spiritual beauty Jesus, as reported by Barnabas, pours out the anguish of his soul to his disciples:

> 'The judgement day of God will be so dreadful that verily I say to you, reprobates would sooner choose ten hells than go to hear God speak in wrath against them, against whom all things will witness. Verily, I say to you that not alone shall the reprobates fear, but the saints and the elect of God, so that Abraham shall not trust in his righteousness, and Job shall have no confidence in his innocence. And what do I say? Even the messenger of God shall fear, for to make known His majesty, God shall deprive His messenger of memory, so that he shall have no remembrance how God has given him all things. *Verily I say to you that speaking from the heart, I tremble because by the world I shall be called a god, and for this I shall have to render an account. As God lives, in whose presence my soul stands, I am a mortal man as are other men, for although God has placed me as a prophet over the house of Israel for the health of the feeble and the correction of sinners, I am the servant of God, and of this you are witness, how I speak against those wicked men who after my departure from the world shall annul the truth of my gospel by the operation of Satan.* But I shall return toward the end, and with me shall come Enoch and Elijah, and we will testify against the wicked, whose end shall be accursed.' And having thus spoken, Jesus shed tears, and his disciples wept aloud, and lifted their voices saying, 'Pardon, O Lord God, and have mercy on your innocent servant.' Jesus answered 'Amen, Amen'(*The Gospel of Barnabas 52*).

The first stage of the fulfillment of his prophecy began in the second year of his prophetic ministry:

> Jesus left Jerasulem in the second year of his prophetic ministry and went to Nain. As he approached the gate of the city, the citizens were bearing to the sepulchre the only son of a mother, a widow, over whom every one was weeping. When Jesus arrived, the men learned that Jesus, a prophet of Galilee, had come, and so they set themselves to beseech him to raise the dead man, which also his disciples did. Then Jesus feared greatly, and turning himself to God, said: 'Take me from the world, O Lord, for the world is mad, and they wellnigh call me God!' And having said this, he wept.

Then the angel Gabriel came and said, 'O Jesus fear not, for God has given you power over every infirmity, and all that you shall grant in the name of God shall be entirely accomplished.' Hereupon Jesus gave a sigh saying, 'Your will be done, Lord God Almighty and Merciful.' And having said this, he drew near to the mother of the deceased, and with pity said to her, 'Woman, weep not.' And having taken the hand of the deceased and, he said, 'I say to you, young man, in the name of God arise up healed!'

Then the boy revived, whereupon all were filled with fear, saying, 'God has raised up a prophet among us, and he has visited his people' (*The Gospel of Barnabas 47*).

The preceding paragraph from *The Gospel of Barnabas* establishes the true meaning of Peter's words: "You men of Israel, hear these words: Jesus of Nazareth, a man approved of God among you by miracles and wonders and signs, which God did by him in the midst of you, as you yourselves also know" (Acts 2:22). Barnabas records the events meticulously:

At that time the army of the Romans was in Judea, our country being subject to them for the sins of our forefathers. Now it was the custom of the Romans to call god and to worship any man who did any thing of benefit to the common people. And so (some) of these soldiers finding themselves in Nain, rebuked the people saying, 'One of your gods has visited you, and you make no account of it. Assuredly if our gods should visit us we should give them all that we have. And you see how much we fear our gods, since to their images we give the best of all we have.' Satan did so instigate this manner of speaking that he aroused no small sedition among the people of Nain. But Jesus tarried not at all in Nain, and turned to go into Capernaum. The discord of Nain was such that some said, 'Our God has visited us; others said, 'God is invisible so that none has seen Him, not even Moses, His servant. Therefore it is not God, but rather His son.' Others said, 'He is not God, nor the son of God, for God does not have a body to beget withal. He is rather a great prophet of God.'

And so did Satan instigate that in the third year of the prophetic ministry of Jesus great ruin to our people was like to arise therefrom.

Jesus went into Capernaum: whereupon the citizens, when they knew him, assembled together all the sick folk they had, and placed them in front of the porch (of the house) where

Jesus was lodging with his disciples. And having called Jesus forth, they implored him for the health of them. Then Jesus laid his hands upon each of them, saying: 'God of Israel, by Your holy name, give health to this sick person.' Whereupon each one was healed (*The Gospel of Barnabas 48*).

The Trinity: A Pagan Expression

In accordance with the Abrahamic religion, the righteous among the Ishmaelite and Israelite worshipped God as the absolute indivisible author of all creation. We are told by the noted Biblical scholar Prof. Foxwell Albright that "there is ample evidence in the Bible that the Israelites had always regarded Yahweh (Jahovah) as the Creator of all. Another original characteristic of the Israelite God was that He stood alone, without any family connections, whether consort, son or daughter."[21] This was not the case with the chief gods of the pagans as Col. J. Garnier points out:

> Our sources of information respecting the ancient paganism are the mythological traditions of Phoenicia, Greece and Rome, the notice of ancient historians, and the researches of modern archaeologists among the monumental remains of Assyria, Egypt, etc.
>
> It is of importance to notice first, that all the various gods and goddesses of the ancients, though known by many names and different characteristics, can yet all be resolved into one of the persons of a Trinity composed of a father, mother and son; and that this fact was well known to the initiated. It should also be observed that the father and the son constantly melt into one; the reason being that there was also a fabled incarnation of the son who, although identified with him, was yet to be his own son by the goddess.[22]

That is why, when Jesus heard himself being called as the Son of God by one of his disciples he became very angry. God to Jesus was unique who had no sons, wives, or daughters. *The Gospel of Barnabas* records the event:

> Jesus departed from Jerusalem after the Passover, and entered into the borders of Caesarea Philippi. There the angel

---

[21] William F. Albright, *From the Stone Age to Christianity*, Doubleday and Co., Inc., Garden City, New York, 1957, p. 261.
[22] Col. J. Garnier, *The Worship of the Dead*, Chapman & Hall, Ltd., 1904, p. 12.

Gabriel having told him of the sedition which was beginning among the common people, he asked his disciples, saying, 'What do men say of me?' They said, 'Some say you are Elijah, others Jeremiah, and others one of the old prophets.'

Jesus asked, 'And you, what do you say that I am?'

Peter answered, 'You are Messiah, Son of God.' Then Jesus was angry, and rebuked him, saying, 'Begone and depart from me, because you are the Devil and seek to cause me offence!'

And he threatened the eleven, saying, 'Woe to you if you believe this, for I have won from God a great curse against those who believe this.'

And he was ready to cast away Peter, but the eleven besought Jesus for him, who did not cast him away, but again rebuked him, saying, 'Beware that you never again say such words, because God would reprobate you.'

Peter wept and said, 'Sir, I have spoken foolishly. Beseech God that He pardons me.'

Then said Jesus, 'If our God willed not to show himself to Moses His servant, nor to Elijah whom he also loved, nor to any prophet, do you think that God should show Himself to this faithless generation? But know you not that God has created all things of nothing with one single word, and all men have had their origin out of a piece of clay? Now, how shall God have a likeness to man? Woe to those who suffer themselves to be deceived of Satan!'

And having said this, Jesus besought God for Peter, the eleven and Peter weeping, and saying, 'So be it, O blessed Lord our God.'

Afterward Jesus departed and went into Galilee in order that this vain opinion which the common folk began to hold concerning him might be extinguished (*The Gospel of Barnabas 70*).

Peter's misidentification of Jesus as being a supposed Son of God, in accordance with Gentile thought, is misrepresented by the Gentiles in the New Testament as having been acceptable to Jesus. See Matthew 16:13-17; Mark 8:27-30; Luke 9:18-21; and John 6:68-69 for further details. Again, in what the Gentiles call the gospel of John, Nathaniel is presented as having said to Jesus, "Rabbi, you are the Son of God, you are the king of Israel," and Martha is presented as having said to Jesus, "I believe that you are the Messiah, the Son of God, he who was to come into the world" (John 1:49; 11:27). In the Greek gospel attributed by them to John, we have an obvious play on words in an attempt to convince the ignorant that Jesus is what the Gentiles believed him to be. But, in misrepresenting Jesus as a deity in the first chapter of John in line with Gnosticism, it contradicts the concept of the Son of God held by the Jews in the Old Testament and used by Matthew in his so-called gospel for Jesus.

As Andrews Norton points out in his commentary to Matthew 3:17 ("This is my beloved Son, with whom I am well pleased."):

> Here may be explained the title 'Son of God' as applied to Christ. The author of the Epistle to the Hebrews (I:5) quotes the words, which God in the Old Testament is represented to have used for Solomon, as applicable to Christ: 'I will be to him a father, and he shall be to me a son.' By these words was meant that God would distinguish Solomon with peculiar favors, would treat him as a father treats a son, and they are to be understood in a similar manner when applied to Christ. 'We beheld,' says St. John in his Gospel (I:.14), 'his glory like that of an only son from a father,' that is, we beheld the glorious powers and offices conferred upon him, by which he was distinguished from all others, as an only son is distinguished by his father. It is in reference to this analogy, and probably, I think, to this very passage in his Gospel, that St. John elsewhere calls Christ 'the only Son of God,' a title applied to him by no other writer of the New Testament.[23]

Norton must have known the historical fact that the Israelites had borrowed from the Canaanite heathenism the expression "sons of God," but used it only as a symbolical expression "to denote those qualities which recommend moral beings to the favor of God; those which bear such a likeness to His moral attributes as may be compared with the likeness which a son has to his father; those which constitute one, in the Oriental (Eastern) style, to be of the family of God." Obviously, misrepresentation of Jesus as a literal Son of God is a gross error.

So pervasive had become the influence of heathenism that even Peter was misled and rightfully received the reprobation from Jesus who rejected this heathen expression. Jesus knew the harm that such heathen expressions were doing and would do in the future. As one who had come to uphold the law of the Prophets, Jesus also knew that such a concept was

---

[23]Andrews Norton, *A Translation of the Gospels*, John Wilson and Son, University Press, 1885, p. 28.

in total violation of the first commandment (Deuteronomy 5:7), and the word of God expressed in Deuteronomy 6:4; Job 33:12; Hosea 11:9; Numbers 23:19; and Genesis 17:17.

Blasphemy and Division in Palestine

After nearly two centuries of resisting Hellenization of their religion and culture, the proclamation by the Hellenized Jews that Jesus was God, or the Son of God, was the last straw that broke the camel's back. The spirit of Judah that ignited the Maccabean revolt against Antiochus IV was now rekindled, and the seekers after righteousness took up arms against the ignorant when they should have taken up the zealous preaching of the word of God:

> At this time there was great disturbance throughout Judea over Jesus, for that the Roman soldiery through the operation of Satan, stirred up the Hebrews, saying that Jesus was God come to visit them. Whereupon so great a sedition arose that for almost forty days all Judea was in arms: son was found against father, and brother against brother, for some said that Jesus was God come to the world, while others said, 'No, but he is a son of God', and others said, 'No, for God has no human likeness and therefore begets not sons. Jesus of Nazareth is only a prophet of God.'
>
> And this arose by reason of the great miracles which Jesus did.
>
> Thereupon, to quiet the people, it was necessary that the high-priest should ride in procession, clothed in priestly robes with the holy name of God, the tetagramaton, on his forehead. And in like manner rode the governor Pilate and Herod.
>
> Three armies assembled in Mizpeh ... Herod spoke to them, but they were not quieted. Then spoke the governor and the high-priest saying, 'Brethren, this war is aroused by the work of Satan, for Jesus is alive, and we ought to resort to him and ask him that he give testimony of himself, and then believe in him, according to his word.'
>
> So at this they were quieted. Having laid down their arms they all embraced one another, saying one to the other, 'Forgive me, brother!'
>
> On that day, accordingly, every one laid it in his heart to believe what Jesus shall say. And by the governor and the high-priest were offered great rewards to him who should come to announce where Jesus was to be found.

At this time, by the word of the holy angel, we with Jesus were gone to Mount Sinai. And there Jesus with his disciples kept the forty days. When this was past, Jesus drew nigh to the river Jordan, to go to Jerusalem. He was seen by one of them who believed Jesus to be God. Over joyed he cried out, 'Our God comes!' Having reached the city, he moved the whole city by saying, 'Our God comes. O Jerusalem! prepare yourself to receive him!' And he testified that he had seen Jesus near the Jordan River.

Then went out from the city every one, small and great, to see Jesus... When they learned of this, the governor and the high-priest rode forth to find Jesus in order that the sedition of the people might be quieted. For two days they sought him in the wilderness near the River Jordan, and on the third day they found him near the hour of midday, when he with his disciples was purifying himself for prayer, according to the book of Moses.

Jesus marvelled greatly, seeing the multitude which covered the gound with people, and said to his disciples, 'Perchance Satan has raised sedition in Judea. May it please God to take away from Satan the dominion which he has over sinners.'

And when he had said this, the crowd drew near, and when they saw him they began to cry out, 'Welcome to you O our God!' and they began to do him reverence, as unto God. Thereupon, Jesus gave a great groan and said, 'Get you from before me, O madmen, for I fear lest the earth should open and devour me with you for your abominable words!' The people were filled with terror and began to weep (*The Gospel of Barnabas 91-92*).

Then Jesus having lifted his hand in token of silence said, 'Verily you have erred greatly, O Israelites, in calling me, a man, your God. And I fear that because of this God may smite the holy city with a heavy plague handing it over in servitude to strangers. May Satan the one who has moved you to this be cursed one thousand times!'

Then Jesus laid his hands upon each of them, saying, 'God of Israel, by Your holy name, give health to this person,' whereupon everyone was healed (*The Gospel of Barnabas 48*).

And having said this, Jesus smote his face with both hands, whereupon arose such a noise of weeping that none could hear what Jesus was saying. He once more lifted up his hand in a token of silence, and the people being quieted from their weeping, he spoke once more: 'I confess before heaven, and I call to witness everything that dwells upon the earth, that I am a stranger to all that you have said, for I am man, born of mortal woman, subject to the judgement of God, suffering the miseries of eating and sleeping, of cold and heat, like other men. When God shall come to judge, my words like a sword shall pierce each one (of them) that believe me to be more than human.

Having said this, Jesus saw a great multitude of horsemen, and he perceived that the governor was coming with Herod and the high-priest.

Then said Jesus, 'Perchance they have also gone insane.'

When the governor arrived with Herod and the priest, every one dismounted, made a circle around about Jesus. The soldiery could not keep back the people who were keen to hear Jesus speaking with the priest.

Jesus drew near to the priest with reverence, but the latter wanted to bow himself down and worship Jesus. Jesus cried out, 'Beware of that which you do, priest of the living God! Sin not against our God!'

The priest answered, 'Now Judea is so greatly moved over your signs and your teaching that they cry out you are God. Thus, forced by the people, I have come here with the Roman governor and King Herod. We pray from our hearts that you will be content to remove the sedition which has arisen on your account. For some say you are God, some say you are son of God, and some say you are a prophet.

Jesus answered, 'And you, O high-priest of God, why have you not quieted this sedition? Have you also, perchance, gone out of your mind? Have the prophecies, with the law of God, so passed into oblivion, O wretched Judea, deceived of Satan!'

Having said this, Jesus said again, 'I confess before heaven, and call to witness everything that dwells upon the earth, that I am a stranger to all that men have said of me, to wit, that I am more than a man. For I am a man, born of a woman, subject to the judgement of God, who lives here as other men, subject to the common miseries. As God lives, in whose presence my soul stands, you have greatly sinned, O priest, in saying what you have said. May it please God that there come not upon the holy city great vengeance for this sin.'

Then said the priest, 'May God pardon us, and do thou pray for us.'

Then said the governor and Herod, 'Sir, it is impossible that man should do that which you do, and because of that we do not understand what you say.'

Jesus answered, 'What you say is true, for God works good in man, even as Satan works evil. For man is like a shop, wherein whoever enters with his consent works and sells therein. But tell me, O governor, and you O king, you say this because you are strangers to our law, for if you read the testament and convenant of our God you would see that Moses made the water turn into blood with a rod, the dust into fleas, the dew into tempest, and the light into darkness. He made the frogs and mice to come into Egypt and cover the ground. He slew the first-born, opened the sea, and drowned the Pharaoh in it. Of these things I have brought none. And Moses, everyone confesses that he is now dead. Joshua made the sun to stand still, and opened the Jordan, which I have not yet done. And of Joshua every one confesses that he is now dead. Elijah made fire to come visibly down from heaven, and rain, which I have not done. And of Elijah every one confesses that he was a man. And (in like manner) many other prophets, holy men, friends of God, who in the power of God wrought things which cannot be grasped by the minds of those who know not our God, Almighty and Merciful, who is blessed for evermore.'

Accordingly the governor and the priest and the king implored Jesus to go up to a lofty place and speak to the people in order to quiet them. Jesus therefore mounted one of the twelve stones which Joshua had made the twelve tribes take up from the midst of Jordan when all Israel passed over there dry shod, and he said with a loud voice, 'Let our priest go up to a high place so that he may confirm my words.' Thereupon, the priest did so and Jesus said to him distinctly so that everyone might hear, 'It is written in the testament and covenant of the living God that our God has had no beginning, neither shall He ever have an end.'

The priest answered, 'Even so is it written therein.'

Jesus said, 'It is written that God is invisible and hidden from the mind of man, for He is incorporeal and uncomposed, without variableness.'

'So is it, truly,' said the priest.

Jesus said, 'It is written there how that the heaven of heavens cannot contain Him, seeing that our God is infinite.'

'So said Solomon the prophet,' said the priest, 'O Jesus.'

Jesus said,'It is written there that God has no need, for He eats not, sleeps not, and suffers not from any deficiency.'

'So is it,' said the priest.

Said Jesus, 'It is written there that our God is everywhere, and that there is not any other god but He, who strikes down and makes whole, and does all that pleases Him.'

'So is it written,' replied the priest.

Then Jesus, having lifted up his hands, 'Lord our God, this is my faith wherewith I shall come to Your judgement in testimony against everyone that shall believe the contrary.' And turning himself toward the people, he said, 'Repent, for all that of which the priest has said that it is written in the book of Moses, the convenant of God for ever, you may perceive your sin because I am a visible man and a morsel of clay that walks upon the earth, a mortal as are other men. I had a beginning and shall have an end, and (am) such that I cannot create a fly over again.'

Thereupon the people raised their voices weeping, and said, 'We have sinned, Lord our God, against You. Have mercy upon us.' And they all implored Jesus that he would pray for the safety of the holy city, that our God in His anger should not give it over to be down trodden of nations. Thereupon Jesus, having lifted up his hands, prayed for the holy city and for the people of God, everyone crying: 'So be it,' 'Amen' (*The Gospel of Barnabas 93-95*).

The Gospel of Barnabas makes it clear that all prophets were assisted by God, who strenghtened them with the Holy Spirit in the discharge of their missions. Jesus was no exception. Like others, he also perfomed miracles. But the miracles have their problems too. Unless performed in the name of God, they lead people to believe that the person performing them has divine attributes. Jesus performed them in the name of God, but the Gentile mind was too willing to invest him with divinity.

In fact, Jesus was not the first to raise the dead (I Kings 17:21; II Kings 4:32; 13:21), nor was he the first to be the product of a virgin birth. As William Smith points out: "Immanuel, that is, God with us, *the symbolical name* given by the Prophet Isaiah to the child who was announced to Ahaz (741-726 BC) and the people of Judah, as the sign which God would give of their deliverance from their enemies (Isaiah 7:14)." He goes on to say: "It would therefore appear that the immediate reference of the prophet was to some *contemporary occurrence.*"[24] In other words, a virgin birth that took place during the time of Ahaz was an unmistakable sign that he and his people would be delivered from the designs of their immediate enemies Rezin King of Damascus and Pekah King of Israel. In the Greek gospel attributed to, but not written by, the Apostle Matthew, the symbolical name Immanuel is applied by its author to the Prophet Jesus, whose birth was also a sign. But the Hellenized Jews and their Gentile masters in their combined ignorance tried to give Jesus' birth a different meaning, and their attempt is fully in accord with the following prophecy spoken by Jesus and recorded in the ninety-sixth chapter of *The Gospel of Barnabas*.

> But when God shall take me away from the world, Satan will raise again this accursed sedition, by making the impious believe that I am God and son of God, whence my words and my doctrine shall be contaminated, so much so that scarcely shall there remain thirty faithful ones.'

Who Were the Nicolaitans?

Evidence derived from the Qumran Scrolls, historical research and *The Gospel of Barnabas* makes it clear that the Trinity is a Gentile innovation.

After his death, Jesus' worst fears were realized when the Nicolaitans, a Gnostic sect condemned in Revelation (2:16 and 15), revived the heresy that Jesus was the son of God. The Nicolaitan sect consisted primarily of Gentiles, but it appears that there were also a number of Jews in it who were obviously Gentiles by culture. It was the Nicolaitans who in opposition to Jesus and his Gospel spread the propaganda that the Nazarenes were not under the obligations of morality. As one recognized source describes them, they were the "Antinomians" of the Apostolic Congregation established by Jesus and his apostles. Now it is important to realize that an Antinomian is one who is opposed to the restrictions of the law. In other words, an Antinomian is a lawless person, no matter how sophisticated he may appear to be. In the case of the Nicolaitans, it is the divine law revealed through the Prophet Moses that they were opposed to. It was because of their fanatical opposition to the Mosaic law that the Nazarenes branded them as the followers of Balaam. "They, like the false prophet of Pethor," says William Smith in his *Bible Dictionary*, "united brave words with evil deeds. In a time of persecution, when the eating or not eating of things sacrificed to idols was more than ever a crucial test of faithfulness, they persuaded men more than ever that it was a thing

---

[24] William Smith Article: Immanuel, op. cit., 253.

indifferent (Revelation 2.13, 14)."[25] An example of their manner of argument is found in I Corinthians where Paul first speaks against the eating of meat sacrificed to idols, and then encourages the eating of such meat:

> But I say that the things which the Gentiles sacrifice, they sacrifice to demons, and not to God; and I would not want you to have fellowship with demons. You cannot drink the cup of the Lord, and the cup of the demons; you cannot partake of the Lord's table, and of the table of the demons...

Now comes the Nicolaitan argument to justify violating the law:

> Or do we provoke the Lord to jealousy? Are we stronger than He? All things are lawful for me, but all things are not expedient; all things are lawful for me, but all things do not edify. Let no one seek his own, but each one the other's well being. Eat whatever is sold in the meat market, asking no questions for conscience sake; for 'The earth is the Lord's, and all its fullness.' If any of those who do not believe invites you to dinner, and you desire to go, eat whatever is set before you, asking no questions for conscience' sake. But if anyone says to you, 'This was offered to idols,' do not eat for the sake of the one who told you, and conscience' sake; for the earth is the Lord's, and all its fullness.' Conscience, I say, not your own, but that of the other. For why is my liberty judged by another man's conscience? But if I partake with thanks, why am I evil spoken of for the food over which I give thanks? Therefore, whether you eat or drink, or whatever you do, do all to the glory of God, just as I also please all men in all things, not seeking my own profit, but the profit of many, that they may be saved.
>
> (I Corinthians 10:20-33).

Here we have a typical use of the esoteric language in which Paul seems to be adept: elusive so as not to offend the true followers and yet permissive for the violators of law.

In Corinthians 8:1-13, we find a more open argument presented by Paul in support of the Nicolaitan conspiracy to encourage Nazarenes, particularly Gentiles who had joined the Nazarene movement, to eat unclean meats in violation of the prohibition against it. Since the

---

[25]Ibid., Article: Nicolaitans, p. 450.

Nicolaitans were against the Gospel of Jesus the Messiah, they were opposed by the apostles and their disciples. This forced them to adopt a cautious approach toward violating the prohibition against the eating of meats sacrificed to idols. Study carefully the insidious manner in which Paul encourages the eating of unclean meats by indicating that he could do it because he was above the Law, which is precisely the Nicolaitan position. As Gnostics, they held the erroneous belief that they were above God's law. These attempts to encourage and justify the eating of unclean meats "was bad enough," says William Smith, "but there was yet a worse evil." [26] Once encouraged to eat meats sacrificed to idols by Paul and other Nicolaitan teachers, the Gentile converts to the Apostolic Congregation more so perhaps than some Hellenized Jewish converts, mingled themselves into the orgies of idolatrous feasts, and brought the impurities of those feasts into their meetings. In other words, the very paganism that Jesus came to purge from the Abrahamic faith was reintroduced into it by the Nicolaitons through these Gentile converts, resulting in the post-exilic system of belief known as Judaism.

For instance, as previously pointed out, the Israelites had borrowed from the Canaanites the term "bene el or bene ha-elohim" meaning "sons of God," which they employed for the angels. But according to Israelite usage, this heathen expression did not mean that they were actually the children of God; both the angels and the Israelites were created by God and as such symbolically might be called His "children", though not literally. Nevertheless, this borrowing from paganism, as we have seen, contributed to the corruption of the faith. Even among the Essenes of Qumran who considered themselves to be the true followers of Abraham and Moses, the belief in the supernatural powers of a coming Messiah to some degree existed. However, it did not result in the kind of belief one finds among the Gentiles. Thus, John Allegro points out that in a Qumran scroll dealing with the Jewish notion of the re-establishment of the Kingdom of David in the Last Days, the prophecy of II Samuel 7:13-14, "I will establish the throne of his kingdom for ever. I will be his father and he shall be my son.," is referred to as the same figure, as it is by the Gentiles in their New Testament (Hebrews 1.5). Allegro goes on to say: "We appear, then, to have in Qumran thought already the idea of the lay Messiah as the Son of God, 'begotten' of the Father, a 'Saviour' in Israel. *At the same time, we nowhere approach the 'christology' of Paul in the Scrolls, or the kind of*

---

[26]Ibid.

divinity accorded Jesus by the Greek Church."[27]

Finally, we find that the (Essenes) of Qumran, nowhere press the erroneous notion of a divinely begotten Son-Messiah and a Co-Existent Holy Spirit to the Gnostic doctrine of a trinitarian godhead as was done by the Nicolaitans.[28] The Rev. Dr. Charles F. Potter explains that in light of a better understanding of the scrolls, the Gentile doctrine of the Holy Spirit as well as that of the Gentile doctrine of the Trinity (the supposed division of the indivisible God of Abraham, Ishmael, Isaac, and Jacob into three distinct personalities) will have to be rejected. One might say that the Gentiles in their naivety have come up with the ridiculous notion of an Almighty God who suffers from a human mental disorder that causes a split personality.

The Origins of the Nicolaitan Heresy

The Greeks, like other pagan nations engaged in agriculture, worshipped the fertillty of the earth in conjunction with the fertility of woman. In fact, the earliest pagan deity of which there is physical evidence seems to have been woman as the childbearer. With the rise of agriculture, female fertility and the fertility of the earth were combined into a composite deity known by many names, but best described as the "earth-mother goddess." In Egypt she was Isis, while in Greece she was known by a variety of names, each one representing a separate deity, such as Aphrodite, Hera, and so on.

With this belief in an earth-mother goddess went the belief in another composite deity, the man-god who in fact personified vegetation and its cycle, and often the sun and its cycle. In the case of Osiris, Baal, and Cronus, he also represented a deceased king worshipped as divine. This man-god, when worshipped in association with the sun, was always supposedly born on *December 25th* so as to correspond with the winter solistice. Forty days later, or around the time of Easter, he had to be *slain,* laid *in a tomb,* and *resurrected* after three days so that his *blood* could be *shed upon the earth* in order to maintain or restore its fertility as well as to ensure the salvation of his worshippers. His resurrection was a sign to them that because he gave his life and shed his blood for them and was resurrected from death, they too would be saved from death and thereby enjoy eternal life. This death and resurrection drama took place so as to correspond with the spring equinox, for in this manifestation of his composite nature he was a sun-god, the sun of righteousness — according to pagan theology. At the

---

[27]John Allegro, *The Dead Sea Scrolls*, Pengiun Books, New York, 1964, pp. 170-171.
[28]Ibid., p. 171.

same time, he was the personification of vegetation which dies and is resurrected from death in the spring.

The worship of the man-god as the symbol of the sun and vegetation cycle, both of which are important to agriculture, and as the symbol of a dead ancestor of great reputation is, in fact, a blend of several mystery beliefs combined into one pagan system. Paganism, through its elaborate rites, brought the person initiated into communion with the man-god. Those persons not belonging to these mystery cults were looked down upon, for it was said that an initiated thief would fare better in the next world than an uninitiated man of good character. And even though writers like Plato condemned these false doctrines and those persons who lived by them, they nevertheless continued to survive and gain devotees, for men then, as now, were concerned about their souls; but too often they were duped by such promoters of false doctrines as the Nicolaitans.

The man-god of these mystery religions based upon the literal worship of the sun, vegetation, and dead ancestors of heroic or unusual deeds, was called the "Soter" in Greece, which means the savior or deliverer. The term itself was sometimes applied to Zeus, the chief god of the Greeks, as "Zeus Soter." The representation of Zeus in ancient Greek theology makes him the epitome of infidelity. Thus, it is not surprising that the idea of an "only-begotten son of god" was common among the Greeks, particularly those who were of the Orphic system of paganism. Such a son, according to their system of belief, was conceived by a mortal woman in some spiritual way, and born as the only begotten son of their god for the salvation of mankind. This pagan system of belief was totally in opposition to the tenets of the Abrahamic religion in which God is worshipped as the supreme, intelligent, and indivisible Creator of all things. After having sunk into paganism at some point in their ancient past as did other nations, the average Greek had no conception of a Creator who had made heaven and earth.

In the Greek system of pagan beliefs, the "Soter" sometimes stood alone, but mostly he was "The Third, the Savior" or "the Savior who is third." Gilbert Murray says in an article that the origin of this conception of a "Soter" rests in the old agricultural cults, "which worshipped and created so many beings to represent the year, or the season, or the vegetation, gods whose coming was the coming of spring or of harvest, and whose annual death was celebrated when the harvest was out or the vegetation died. The god had been killed — most often torn in pieces and scattered over the fields — by a second being, his enemy, through whose victory the life of the earth seemed dead, till there came a third being, a saviour who slew the enemy and brought back the dead god, or was himself the dead god restored."[29]

In some of the earliest and most savage expressions of the agriculture cult, the climax of ecstatic worship was supposed to bring the worshipper into "communion," to make him one with his god, that is, to make him part of the body. Where a real king was slain as the god incarnated into human form so as to walk upon the earth as man and god, actual cannibalism and vampirism was practiced. The "holy communion," as they believed, involved eating his flesh and drinking of that portion of his blood which had not been spilled upon the ground. In time, the savage feast underwent a change, in that the literal form of savagery was replaced with a symbolic form. Wine or some other such beverage symbolizing blood was consumed as the god-king's blood, along with bread, symbolizing his flesh. An example of this same barbarity in the Egyptian agriculture or the Osirian cult, is reported by Margaret A. Murray:

> Even as late as the Ptolemies, the killing of a god was still practised, though that god was called the enemy of Osiris. And though the figure of the god was probably made only of bread, the worshippers were still called to the cannibal feast: "Eat ye the flesh of the vanquished, drink ye his blood."[30]

Some of the Gnostic sects replaced even this symbolic expression of savagery with a communion involving ecstasy and contemplation. For to "know" the god that they worshipped meant in this context, to be made one with him (Gnosis= knowledge). This was not so with the Nicolaitans, who still practised the symbolic form of this savage feast. Consider the fact that even though the Greek document known as "The Gospel according to John" says that the bones of Jesus were not broken, Paul in I Corinthians contradicts this by putting words into Jesus' mouth in an attempt to justify the Nicolaitan introduction of the cannibal feast into what became the Christian Church. In the Greek document attributed by them to John the son of Zebedee, it is said:

Christian Church. In the Greek document attributed by them to John the son of Zebedee, it is said:

> But when they came to Jesus and saw that he was already dead, they broke not his legs. But one of the soldiers pierced His side with a spear, and immediately blood and water came

---

[29]History of Christianity In the Light of Modern Knowledge, A Collective Work, Harcourt, Brace & Co., New York, p. 70.

[30]Margaret A. Murray, The Splendour That was Egypt, Sidg Wickt Jakson, Ltd., London, 1949, p. 168.

out. And he who has seen has testified, and his testimony is true; and he knows that he is telling the truth, so that you may believe. For these things were done that the scripture should be fulfilled, 'Not one of his bones shall be broken' (John 19:33-36).

Now compare this with the following contradiction in Paul's epistle to the Corinthians:

> For I received from the Lord that which I also delivered to you: that the Lord Jesus on the same night in which He was betrayed took bread; and when he had given thanks, He broke it, and said, 'Take, eat; this is my body which is broken for you; do this in remembrance of Me.' In the same manner He also took the cup, after supper, saying, 'This cup is the new covenant in my blood. This do, as often as you drink it, in remembrance of Me. For as often as you eat this bread and drink this cup, you proclaim the Lord's death till He comes (I Corinthians 11:23-26).

The Nicolaitan Heresy

How far the Nicolaitans succeeded in paganizing Jesus' faith can be read in the trinitarian doctrine of the Gnostic, which was adopted by the Church in AD 325:

> We believe in one God, the Father all-Sovereign, maker of all things, both visible and invisible:
> And in one Lord Jesus Christ, the Son of God, begotten of the Father, an only begotten;
> That is, from the essence of the Father,
> God from God, Light from Light, true God from true God-begotten, not made — being of one essence with the Father;
> By whom all things were made, both things in heaven and things on earth;
> Who for us men and for our salvation came down and was made flesh, was made man, suffered, and rose again the third day, ascended into heaven, cometh to judge the quick and the dead:
> And in the Holy Spirit.

The Scrolls, The Gospel of Barnabas, and New Testament 55

But those who say that 'there was once when he was not,' and before he was begotten he was not,' and 'he was made of things that were not,' or maintain that the Son of God is of a different essence, or created or subject to moral change or alteration — these doth the Catholic and Apostolic Church anathematize.[31]

To say "God from God" is the reformulation of the pagan belief that there are more than one God, and that he procreates. Again "true God from true God" stresses the same Gnostic thought that a god proceeded from God. This is what we have in one of the Greek gospels:

In the beginning was the *Word,* and the *Word* was *with God,* and the Word was God. He was in the beginnning with God
(John 1:1-2).

Count them: God, and the Word, two deities, not one, and not three. Wnat we have here is not monotheism, (the worship of one God), nor trinitarianism (the worship of three gods, or God, and two false gods), but rather a form of dualism in which God and a false god are acknowledged. Ironically, the so-called gospel of John that the Gentiles so often invoke to support their cherished doctrine of the Trinity, in fact, negates it. The diehards may still point to 1 John 5:7 as the best statement on the Trinity, but ironically that verse, as stated by Charles F. Potter, is "... a forgery, a deliberate interpolation, said by some to have crept in from a marginal note. Recognized as such, it was eliminated by the English revisers in 1881, by Moffat, Goodspeed, and the edition of recent Revised Standard version." Both the Rheims (Catholic) and King James versions retain this forgery in their text. But the New Scofield Reference Edition of the KJV in its commentary admits the spurious nature of I John 5:7, and 5:13. The Confraternity (Episcopal-Catholic) version, though it too retains it in its text, does make the following admission: "According to the evidence of many manuscripts and the majority of the commentators, the verse should not be included."

Nevertheless, it is with the addition of "Sophia" (Divine Wisdom) as the Holy Spirit that the Nicolaitans formulated their triad of three deities. For, like the god that supposedly proceeded from God, the Holy Spirit of the Gnostic creed of the Nicolaitans presented here was also a deity. Notice,

---

[31] Joseph Campbell, *The Masks of God: Accidental Mythology*, Penguin Books, New York, 1976, p. 389.

how in this official proclamation of the Christian version of the Trinity, the nature of the Holy Spirit is not explained, even though it is one of the three deities. Now consider also their misrepresentation of Melchizdek as a deity, for although only the true God exists without a beginning or end (Genesis 21:33), the Christians are told in Hebrews 7:1-3 that Melchizdek is also an eternal being: "For this Melchizdek, king of Salem, priest of the Most High God, who met Abraham returning from the slaughter of the kings, and blessed him, to whom also Abraham gave a tenth part of all; first being, by interpretation, king of righteousness, and after that also king of Salem, which is king of peace; *without father, without mother, without descent, having neither beginning of days nor end of life*, but made like unto the Son of God, abideth a priest continually." If this is not polytheism, what is?

In accordance with the Gnostic attitude of hostility toward the God of Abraham, Ishmael, Isaac, and Jacob (Israel), Paul in his letter to the Galatians falsely belittles Ishmael (meaning "he whom the Lord God will hear") and his mother (Galatians 4:21-31). The Israelites, particularly the true followers of Jesus' Gospel, though he does not mention them by name, are repeatedly spoken against by him in his epistles.

> There is therefore now no condemnation to those who are in Christ Jesus, who do not walk according to the flesh, but according to the spirit. For the law of the Spirit of life in Christ Jesus has made me free from the law of sin and death. For what the law could not do, in that it was weak through the flesh, God did by sending His own Son, in the likeness of sinful flesh, on account of sin: He condemned sin in the flesh, that the righteous requirement of the law might be fulfilled in us who do not walk according to the flesh but according to the spirit.

The Nicolaitans being against God, and therefore against His law, falsely portrayed His law as being burdensome and meaningless in the attainment of salvation. This is the very essence of Paul's arguments in Romans, I Corinthians, and so on. He openly declared himself to be above the law of God, and therefore not restricted by its tenets in his behavior (I Corinthians 10:23). By his arguments, he makes an open declaration that he is in fact a Nicolaitan. The true followers of Jesus' Gospel were striving in accordance with God's will to be obedient to Him by striving to be obedient to His law. As William Smith admits in his *Bible Dictionary* that once the Gentiles were allowed into the Apostolic Congregation the great controversy whether or not the Gentile converts will have to strive as diligently as the Jewish converts in submitting to God's law was inevitable.

Smith then unwittingly goes on to reveal the Nicolaitan misrepresentation of this episode. For the truth of the matter is that all Nazarenes were to be governed by the law of God. This is why the authentic apostles opposed Paul as they opposed the rest of the Nicolaitans — a subject we will discuss later.

THE GNOSTIC ORIGIN
OF THE CHRISTIAN CHURCH

The Ebionites as a Sect Distinct from the Nazarenes

One of the important differences between early believers in Jesus' ministry was their conception of his anointment. The issue of illumination, and his reception of it, became a critical one.

Within the ancient Judaic manuscripts known as The Dead Sea Scrolls or the Qumran Scrolls resides the formidable *Manual of Discipline*. Believed to have belonged to the Essene Movement, with which Jesus was presumably involved, it prescribes an invocation for illumination to initiates of their brotherhood:

> Then the priests are to invoke a blessing on all that have chosen to serve God, that walk blamelessly in all their ways; and they are to say: May He bless thee with all good and keep thee from all evil, and illumine thy heart with insight into the things of life, and grace thee with knowledge of things eternal, and *lift up his gracious countenance towards thee* to grant peace everlasting.[32]

The preceding reading clearly defines illumination and the totality of spiritual life as a very personal experience. The relationship between God and man is stated as direct, without intermediary. With this background, it became inevitable that Jesus should have the experience he reported to Barnabas:

> Jesus, having come to the age of thirty years, as he himself said to me, went up to Mount Olivet with his mother to gather olives. At midday as he was praying, when he came to these words: 'Lord, with mercy ...,' he was surrounded by an

---

[32]Theodor H. Gaster, op. cit., p. 47.

exceedingly bright light and by an infinite multitude of angels, who were saying: 'Blessed be God.' The angel Gabriel presented to him as it were a shining mirror, a book, which descended into the heart of Jesus, in which he had knowledge of what God has done and what God has said, and what God willed, insomuch that everything was laid bare and open to him. He said to me: 'Believe, Barnabas, that I know every prophet with every prophecy, so much so that whatever I say the whole has come forth from that book.'

Jesus, having received this vision, and knowing that he was a prophet sent to the house of Israel, revealed all to Mary his mother, telling her that he must suffer great persecution for the honor of God, and that he could not any longer abide with her to serve her. Having heard this, Mary answered: 'Son, ever since you were born all was announced to me. Blessed be the holy name of God.' Jesus departed therefore that day from his mother to attend to his prophetic office (*The Gospel Of Barnabas 10*).

From the preceding it is obvious that Jesus' heart was illuminated with things eternal. The *Manual Of Discipline,* which is believed to have belonged to the Essene movement, mentions it; but *The Gospel of Barnabas*, as the illumination pertained to Jesus, describes it.

Ebionites, a sect which was significant as an intermediate step between the Nazarenes and the Christians (the victims of the Nicolaitan conspiracy), had a different view about the official beginning of Jesus' mission. Their adoptionist viewpoint is perhaps best portrayed for us in the gospel wrongly attributed to Matthew:

> Then Jesus came from Galilee to John at the Jordan, to be baptized by him. And John tried to prevent him, saying, 'I have need to be baptized by you and you are coming to me?' But Jesus answered and said to him, 'Permit it to be so now, for thus it is fitting for us to fulfill all righteousness. Then he allowed him. Then Jesus, when he had been baptized, came up immediately from the water; and behold, the heavens were opened to him, and he saw the Spirit of God descending like a dove, and alighting upon him. And suddenly a voice came from heaven, saying, 'This is my beloved Son, in whom I am well pleased' (Matthew 3:13-17).

Like the Nazarenes, the Ebionites were ascetics attempting to reach back to the "old Arabian life" of the Patriarchs. Although they are known to have flourished between the first and fourth century, the prominence given by them to John suggests that they, at some point in time prior to the first century, were a legitimate sect of John's followers. For despite patristic mention of an Ebion as their founder, the word "Ebionites" actually refers to the "poor men," which may or may not link them to the "poor" (ebjonim) stated in the sixteenth chapter of *The Gospel Of Barnabas* from which it filtered into Matthew 5:3, Luke 4:18, and 7:22. The Ebionites are reported to have emigrated from Palestine to Transjordan and Syria. Like the Nazarenes and Sadocites of the Qumran tradition, they opposed the corrupted form of the Abrahamic religion — the popular Judaism of their day.

The prominence of John the Baptist in Ebionite thought is obvious. They saw him as spiritually qualified by virtue of his strict ascetic life to baptize Jesus and thus make him accepted by God as His spiritually adopted son. According to their way of thinking, it is from them that Jesus and his followers came. In other words, the Ebionites were esoterically making the claim that they superseded the Nazarenes as the servants of God by having patterned themselves after John the Baptist. They looked upon Jesus as the Israelite Messiah because of his pre-eminent virtue. Only by John's anointment, according to them, was Jesus accepted by God as His adopted son. Contrary to the Nicolaitans, they do not exceed the limits of the Abrahamic religion by ascribing divinity to Jesus as the supposed literal son of God. Nevertheless, they come dangerously close by falling back on the adoptionist viewpoint (II Samuel 7:1-14, concerning Solomon). After all, the Canaanite expression "son of God" had been in the Jewish usage for centuries.

Ebionites' Opposition to Paul the First Christian

Paul of Tarsus, who has the dubious distinction of being recognized as the first Christian, was staunchly opposed by both the Nazarenes and the Ebionites as an enemy of the true Gospel of Jesus. The Ebionites violently opposed the Nicolaitan inspired theology of Paul, and maintained that his alleged vision on the road to Damascus was a demonical hallucination, and that Paul had opposed the conversion of the Jews to a more perfect observance of the Mosaic law through adherence to the authentic Gospel of Jesus.[33]

The Ebionites maintained that Paul was literally the son of a Greek mother and father and therefore could not have been an Israelite. If this is true, then they may well have been "God-fearers" — Gentiles who believed in the one true God, and who saw the gods they had been serving as no more than insensate idols. The true nature of heathen gods was a

---

[33] *The New Catholic Encyclopedia* Article: Ebionites, McGraw Hill Book Co., 1967, p. 34.

theme the synagogues were always stressing. They proclaimed that pagan gods were not gods at all, even the noblest and most benevolent of them, according to the doctrines of their devotees. The Ebionites further maintained that after spending some time in Jerusalem Paul got himself circumcised because he wished to marry into the family of the Jewish High Priest. When rejected, in part perhaps because of the Jewish law against marrying Gentiles, he turned apostate in retaliation and began to attack the law of the Jews.[34]

Evidence in support of the Ebionite claim that Paul was of Gentile ancestry comes from historical research. Paul's claim that he was born a Jew and brought up at the feet of Rabbi Gamaliel (Acts 22:3; 26:5) is dubious to say the least. Gamaliel's pupils were youthful law students who were so well-educated in the Pentateuch, the Prophets, and the Oral Tradition, that they could comprehend and benefit by Rabbi Gamaliel's post-graduate instruction. Paul's epistle reveals but a smattering of synagogue education, and even that is Greek, not Hebrew, in nature. As pointed out in the *Nazarene Gospel Restored,* all his quotations from the Old Testament are based on the *Septuagint,* even where its text wrongly diverges from the Hebrew original. The *Septuagint,* which was a somewhat inaccurate Greek translation of the Jewish Scriptures (with their discrepancies), was current at that time. In the same work, it is further explained that Paul had a grounding in Greek philosophy, but that nowhere in his writings does he quote Zeno or Cleanthes, as one would expect an educated Tarsian to do. His language and style demonstrate that Greek and not Hebrew was his first language, even though his syntax is faulty. In other words, when Paul said that he was rude in speech (II Corinthians 11:6), he was admitting that he was a poorly educated man by any standards. Therefore, it is obvious that he could not have been one of Rabbi Gamiliel's young law students at any time. In I Corinthians, Paul claims to have been a Jew. But among the Gentiles, he does not claim to have remained a Jew.[35] In fact, he fits the description of a "God-fearer" rather than of a Hellenized Jew. The "God-Fearer" generally speaking, were Gentiles who were unwilling to become new converts to Judaism, partly because of the requirement of circumcision, which they thought was a form of mutilation and would affect their manhood, and partly because they did not wish to join the Jewish nation. They, nevertheless,

---

[34]A. Powell Davies, *The First Christian,* Farrar, Straus & Cudhay, New York, 1957, p. 113.
Robert Graves and Joshua Podro, *The Nazarene Gospel Restored,* Doubleday & Co., Inc., 1954, p. 764.
[35]Ibid., p. 765.

were constant in their attendance at the synagogue where they stood in the back because they were still uncircumcised. Here they could learn much concerning Jewish teachings, all of which lends credibility to the Ebionite charge that Paul was a Greek pretending to be a Jew.

Paul's credibility is further damaged by his partial admission in Galatians that his conversion story is fictional. His admission, along with the numerous discrepancies in his story, raises a very serious question: What really happened on the road to Damascus to this earliest, most well-known teacher of Christianity, if anything? Now compare the following three accounts: Acts 9:3-7; Acts 22:6-9; and Acts 26:12-15.

The first account says:

> And as he journeyed he came near Damascus, and suddenely a light shone around him from heavan. Then he fell to the ground, and heard a voice saying to him, 'Saul, Saul, why are you persecuting Me?' And he said,'Who are you, Lord?' And the Lord said, 'I am Jesus, whom you are persecuting. It is hard for you to kick against the goads.' So he, trembling and astonished, said, 'Lord, what do you want me to do?' And the Lord said to him, 'Arise and go into the city, and you will be told what you must do.' And the men who journeyed with him stood speechless, *hearing a voice* but seeing no one. Then Saul arose from the ground, and when his eyes were opened he saw no one. But they led him by the hand and brought him into Damascus (Acts 9:3-8).

In the preceding account, Jesus is made to reply: "*I am Jesus*, whom you are persecuting." We are also told that "the men who were journeying with Paul stood speechless, *hearing the voice* but seeing no one."

In the second telling of the tale, it says:

> Now it happened, as I journeyed and came near Damascus at about noon, suddenly a great light from heavan shone around me. I fell to the ground and heard a voice saying to me, 'Saul, Saul, why are you persecuting Me?' So I answered,'Who are you, Lord? And He said to me, '*I am Jesus of Nazareth*, whom you are persecuting.' Now those who were with me indeed saw the light and were afraid, *but they did not hear the voice of Him who spoke to me* (Acts 22:6-9).

In the preceding account, which is the second telling of the tale, Jesus is made to reply: "I am Jesus of Nazareth," and not just Jesus contrary to the first tale. Second, the men with him see the light but they don't hear the

64   The Gnostic origin of the Christian Church

voice, which is again contrary to the first account, where the men also hear the voice.

In the third telling of the tale, it says:

> While thus occupied, as I journeyed to Damascus with authority and commission from the chief priests, at midday, O king, along the road I saw a light from the heavan, brighter than the sun, shining around me and those who journeyed with me. And when *we all had fallen to the ground, I heard a voice speaking to me* and saying in the Hebrew language...(Acts 26:12-14).

In the preceding account, which is the third telling of the tale, we are told that Paul and his companions all fell to the ground. As one can see, Paul contradicts his previous two accounts in the following way:

> All of them (except Paul) stood speechless, hearing the voice but seeing no one.
> All of them saw the light, but except Paul none heard the voice.
> All of them saw the light and they fell to the ground.

But this is not all to Paul's story. The conversion aspect of his account is equally riddled with contradictions. In Act 9:10-15, we are told that Ananias was sent *by Jesus to commission Paul to be an apostle* to the Gentiles, kings, and Israelites. In Acts 22:10-15, we are told that Jesus in a *vision* sent Paul into Damascus where he would be *told* what it was that he was to do, and that it was Ananias, a devout man of the law, who directly commissioned him. But in Acts 26:16-18 we are told that Jesus commissioned Paul himself *right* there on the road to Damascus. All three accounts, in light of these and other discrepancies, seriously contradict each other as to how Paul was allegedly converted to the Nazarene movement and commissioned to be an apostle. The Ebionite claim that Paul had a demonic inspired hallucination derives support by the statement that "Saul (Paul) arose from the ground, and when his eyes were opened, he saw no one. But they led him by the hand, and brought him into Damascus. And he was three days without sight, and neither ate nor drank" (Acts 9:8-9).

In light of this blindness attributed to the experience Paul had on the road to Damascus, it is no wonder that the Ebionites dismissed Paul's alleged vision as a demonic inspired hallucination. For Moses, Aaron, and Hagar witnessed within human limits the glory of God (Exodus 3:1-6; 19:19-24; and Genesis 16:13), and none of them was blinded for any length of time. Yet we are told that Paul lost his sight for three days after seeing not God, mind you, but Jesus. Paul's statement in his epistle to the Galatians strongly implies that he never regained full use of his sight (Galatians 4:13-15). It has been suggested by some writers that Paul was brooding over the death of Stephen, which deeply affected him, when he suddenly had some kind of traumatic experience, perhaps an epileptic seizure, or he fell on the ground because of the heat of the sun, which caused him to believe in his troubled mind that he heard the voice of Jesus reproaching him for his deeds.

The key to Paul's vision and conversion story on the road to Damascus lies in his statement in I Corinthians 15:8, "...then last of all He (Jesus) was seen by me also, as by one born out of due time." To understand what he is really saying, we must go back to the fact that he thought and spoke as a Nicolaitan, having embraced their doctrines which were deeply rooted in the pagan thought of his day.

The Modernization of Paganism

In the ancient world of pagan thought, there were two chief forms of dualism, both of which contributed to the doctrines of the Nicolaitans. The first pagan belief to be considered here comes from Hermes Trismegistos "the thrice-great Hermes," the Greek title for Thoth, the ancient Egyptian god of wisdom. In this system of belief, the sun was regarded as the creator. By the word sun, the expositors and philosophers adhering to the Hermetic system of beliefs maintained that the latent cause of all creation, vegetation, and motion was the solar fire. This is why the ancient pagan writers identified their gods with the sun. As Godfrey Higgins explains: "Diodorus Siculus says that it was the belief of the ancients that Osiris, Serapis, Dionusos, Pluto, Jupiter, and Pan, were all one." Also Nonnus said that all the different gods, whatever might be their names, Hercules, Ammon, Apollo, or Mithra, "centered in the Sun." According to Higgins, Selden says: "Whether they be called Osiris, or Omphis, or Nilus, or Siris, or by any other name, they all centre in the Sun, the most ancient deity of the nations (Gentiles)".[36]

To them, the sun was the life-giving fire, the principle of heat expanded throughout all nature, without which matter would have remained forever buried in chaos. To them, the generation of bodies was the result of the action and reaction of their constituent parts. They went on to declare that since nature works by fermentation, and fermentation demonstrates on the face of it two powers, one single force, one single principle, one single

---

[36]Godfrey Higgins, *Anacalypsis, Vol.I* University Books, New York, 1965, pp. 44-45.

active cause could never have given energy and life to the universe. Therefore they contended, there could not be one Creator rather there must be two creators, two primate priniciples which had worked out the development from chaos. Since they were aware of the original human couple that was responsible for the initial reproduction of humankind, they incorporated it into their dualism. It was their contention that since everything in the universe is only fire or water, humid or warm, the male principle was fiery and active and the female principle humid and passive. According to the Hermetic doctrines, the male was Form, Heaven, or Sun, while the female was Matter, Earth or the Moon. These two principles were the supposed originators of all things in existence. As all of the chief gods of the pagans during the popular era of this doctrine were but representations of the sun, all of the goddesses were but representations of the female principle symbolized by the moon, or earth. This is also why the "great goddess," as Col. J. Garnier calls her, was called "Dea Myrionymus" — "the goddess with ten thousand names."[37]

The real basis of the Hermetic system of belief was nothing more than the old agriculture cult mentioned in the previous chapter. In other words, it was nothing more than a modernized form of the worship of fertility in man and nature, symbolized by the sun and moon, heaven and earth, matter and form. On the other hand, the other dualism that was popular and influential enough to influence Nicolaitan thought was Magianism.

The concept of God (Ahura Mazda), "The All-Wise Lord," was retained from the teachings of Zarathustra. According to Magianism, Ahura Mazda was the Creator of everything except moral and physical evil, which was created by Aingra Mainyu (Ahriman the Demon). Thus as Gerald L. Barry points out : "The spirit of good was Ahura Mazda, Lord of Wisdom, with his helper, Mithra, Light." Mithra was worshipped as a deity among the Aryan branch of the Japhethinians (Indo-Europeans). Mithra appears both in the Avesta of the Magians and the Rigveda of the Hindus. Mithra was the sun, and therefore identifiable with the male principle of Hermeticism. Zarathustra seems to have discarded in his teachings a significant portion of Persian idolatry, if not all of it. Nevertheless, in time Mithra re-emerged within Magianism as the chief minister of God, supposedly "sent by God to keep watch over the world." Keeping this in mind, let us now see how this was incorporated into Gnosticism.

Drawing upon these and similar thought patterns, the Gnostics developed their own elaborations that took on many forms. These were

---

[37] Col. J. Garnier, op. cit., p. 13.

exceedingly elaborate on the surface, but their internal form was the same old cult of agriculture. It was their belief that the composite god, their chief deity, was far above earthly life and had taken no interest in it. They also thought that there had been, before the beginning of time, an original heavenly man who had been composed of nothing but light (Mithra was supposedly composed of nothing but light), and that the demonic powers of darkness (or a creator god, or world soul aeon) or combination of world souls had conquered this man of light, who was the prototype of mankind, and had broken him up into millions of tiny particles of light which they (or he) had used as magnetic forces to create the world out of the chaos of darkness.

In the Isis-Osiris version of the cult of agriculture, a myth was created to explain in a coded form the introduction of new forms of agriculture into ancient Egypt. In this myth, upon which the preceding Gnostic myth was built, the god of fertility is credited with the introduction of new forms of agriculture. His death by asphyxiation, his dismemberment, and the burial of the fragments of his body in the earth gave rise to the notion of the fragmented man of light.

In their further mystification of the cult of agriculture, it was said by the Gnostics that the sparks of light must be closely guarded by the demons, because if the sparks were removed and reunited, the world would go back to chaos. Thus, they believed that great numbers of demons throughout the heavens and the planets kept watch over these sparks of light by maintaining outposts. From these outposts, the demons along with Destiny exercised control over mankind. The basis of this teaching was the myth found in the Isis-Osirian cult: Isis collected the fragments of the body of "Osiris the Redeemer," and raised a cenotaph (an empty tomb) in each place where the fragments were found. Isis and the goddess Nephthys united the fragments of Osiris' body and by their magic power restored life to the body so that the god Osiris arose from the dead. Osiris was thus the god of the dead and of the ressurection (of plant life) typified as the grain which is buried and sprouts to life from the ground. He was also the "Savior," who died for the salvation of mankind. Mithra was associated with Osiris to the point that Isis, the wife-mother of Osiris, was made the virgin mother of Mithra the god of light.

A further basis for the preceding myth was the Greek belief rooted in Platonic and Orphic thought: *"sooma seema,"* meaning, "the body, a tomb." It was their belief that at death the immortal ethereal human being was freed from the material body and had the opportunity to escape to that non-material world to which it rightly belonged. Thus, the Gnostics maintained that in the case of earthly man, the particles of light guarded by the demons was man's innermost self (it would be incorrect to say soul) and it kept man more or less troubled, yearning to return to heaven, which was his home. To keep this longing under control, the demons kept man in a drugged stupor — he sometimes forgot heaven and at other times remembered it and longed for deliverance from his earthly prison.

The Gnostics further thought that their chief deity eventually became aware of what the demons were up to, and moved by compassion at the sad condition of man, sent his son to save mankind. Here we have the typical pagan concept of a "son of god." Says Col. J. Garnier:

> It should also be observed that the father (god) and the son (of god) constantly melt into one; the reason being that there was a fabled incarnation of the son, who, although identified with him, was yet said to be his own son by the goddess mother. Hence being the father of this supposed incarnation of himself, he was naturally sometimes confused with the original father of the gods, the result of which was that both father and son were sometimes called by the same name.

This is precisely the situation in Christianity, thanks to the Nicolaitans who have the Christians calling God Jesus, and Jesus God (John 1:1-2).

In the Gnostic system, the son of the god they worshipped is carefully disguised in an earthly body so that the demons will not recognize him. In misidentifying Jesus with this pagan redeemer, Paul declares: "But we speak the wisdom of God in a mystery, the hidden *wisdom* which God ordained before the ages for our glory, which none of the rulers of this age knew; for had they known, they would not have crucified the Lord of glory" (I Corinthians 2:7-8). As Prof. Brandon points out, the words *"archontes tou aionos toutou"* properly translated in the New Scofield Reference Edition of the Bible, as "princes (or rulers) of this age" do not refer, as is erroneously believed, to the Roman and Jewish authorities, who were responsible for condemning Jesus to death. They instead refer to the demons, who were associated with the planets in the Gnostic system of belief, and who were believed to be the governors of the human lives on earth. This indicates that the Gnostics had incorporated astrology into their pagan religious system. Prof. Brandon explains: "In this passage (Corinthians 2:7-8) then, Paul is found explaining that before the beginning of a series of world-ages God determined to send into the world, for the good of mankind, a pre-existent divine being, whom the daemonic rulers of the world, not perceiving his real nature, put to death and thereby in some way confounded themselves."[38]

---

[38] S.G.F. Brandon, *Religion in Ancients History,* Charles Scribner's Sons, New York, 1969, pp. 326-327.

In the older Gnostic systems we find that the pagan redeemer is to go about preaching and healing. The redeemer has, however, another mission: he gives to the elect the supposedly sacred passwords which they will need in their journey through space where the demonic powers maintained their outposts. The Savior was to go before them to mark the way, passing through a series of "heavens" until he reached the father-god. There he waits while each of "his own" at death ascends to meet him. Finally, and this is the undoing of the demons, all the sparks of light would then be reassembled to restore the heavenly man, and the material world would fall back into chaos.

In his misidentification of Jesus with the pagan redeemer, Paul insinuates him to be one and the same with Mithra (the god of light as portrayed in Gnosticism), whose glory was so great that he, Paul, was blinded by it. This is the significance of his blindness due to his reported vision of Jesus on the road to Damascus. This is also why he defines his apostleship in Gnostic terminology. Jesus appeared to him, he says, as by "one born out of due time"; to translate literally, as to "the abortion" (I Corinthians 15:8). "This phrase is incomprehensible," says Rev. Dr. Davies, "until we know that according to the Gnostic cosmogny the abortion is the surplus of crude matter which had been cast out of the cosmos when it was created but which was used by the Gnostic Saviour to form a perfect 'Aeon' or (very roughly) 'world-soul'".[39] What Paul is trying to convince the Corinthians of is that his apostleship came to him late or under humbler conditions than in the case of the authentic apostles of Jesus the Messiah, and that his Savior, the Gnostic Savior (Soter), whom he misidentified with Jesus, had especially "formed" him out of the "material" rejected when creating the other apostleships so as to make him (Paul) the perfect apostle.[40]

The discrepancies in Paul's story are now understandable. It was invented by a Gentile, or Gentiles (or a Jew with a Gentile mind) after he became a Nicolaitan to legitimize his self-proclaimed apostleship to the Gentiles.

**Paul's inadvertant Admission that
He was Guilty of Fabrication**

Upon a closer look then, important facets of Paul's apostleship, as reported by him, have easily lent themselves to an informed reappraisal of fact versus fiction.

Another story which easily makes one wonder is Paul's assertion of

---

[39] A. Powell Davies, op. cit., pp. 120-122.
[40] Ibid.

empowerment to make arrests in a foreign city. We are told he had obtained warrants from the high priest of Jerusalem for fugitives living in Syrian cities. Though reportedly accompanied by a patrol of armed guards, it is difficult to believe that he would be allowed to march armed guards through a foreign city's gates, make arrests and carry off prisoners without the objections and interference of the native authorities. In analogy, Russian authorities would surely prevent the US from pursuing political refugees into their nation with a show of force.

However, the most damaging discrepancy comes from Paul's own hand. In different sections of the New Testament, varying accounts of his life and mission after the Damascus Road incident beg comparison and analysis.

In the first version, Paul escapes from Damascus, goes to Jerusalem and is finally admitted to the community of believers by the apostles after Barnabas convinces them to do so. In Acts 9:28-29 it is said: "So, he was with them, at Jerusalem coming in and coming out and he boldly spoke in the name of the Lord Jesus and disputed against the (Hellenists), but they attempted to kill him".

In the second version, a riot breaks out before he can reach this point in the telling of the tale.

In the third version (Acts 26:19-20), Paul says, "Therefore, King Agrippa, I was not disobedient to the heavenly vision, but declared first to those in Damascus, and in Jerusalem, and throughout all the region of Judea and then to the Gentiles, that they should repent, turn to God, and do works befitting repentance."

As Rev. Dr. Davies points out, "These assertions are not inconsistent with each other, but are damaging for another reason: they are contradicted by Paul himself in his letter to the Galatians (chaps. 1 & 2): 'But when it pleased God, who seperated me from my mother's womb, and called me through His grace to reveal His Son in me that I might preach Him among the Gentiles, I did not immediately confer with flesh and blood nor did I go up to Jerusalem to those who were apostles before me, but I went to Arabia, and returned again to Damascus. Then, after three years, I went up to Jerusalem to see Peter and remained with him fifteen days. I saw no other apostles except James, the Lord's brother'" (Galatians 1:15-19). Paul, as Rev. Dr. Davies says, interposes here an oath in the text of his letter: "Now concerning the things which I write to you, indeed, before God I do not lie" (Galatians 1:20), which makes his account of the tale an affidavit. And continuing, Paul says, "Afterwards I went into the regions of Syria and Cilicia, and I was *unknown by face* to the *churches of Judea* which were in Christ" (Galatians 1:21-22).[41]

---

[41] A. Powell Davies, op. cit., pp. 26-32.

"To the story in Acts," explains Dr. Davies, "this contradiction is disastrous. There never was a preaching campaign at Jerusalem and through all the country of Judea (Acts 26:20). If Paul was unknown to the Judean communities as he says, then he had undertaken no mission among them. In fact, he had never joined the Judean movement or even attempted to join it. He saw only Cephas (Peter) and Jesus' brother James. Even of the other apostles, not to mention more ordinary believers, 'I saw none 'he admits. Instead of his having gone 'in and out at Jerusalem, preaching boldly in the name of the Lord,' the Jerusalem community had not even known that he was there. 'They only heard,' he tells us, 'that he who once persecuted us now preaches the faith of which he made havoc'; but they never heard him preach it in Judea."[42]

Therefore, if Paul can be believed about anything, Barnabas had not convinced, or even attempted to convince the apostles at Jerusalem to accept Paul as a new convert and member of the Nazarene movement, as the author of Acts would have us believe. According to Paul's own testimony, he had never been a Nazarene. As the Rev. Dr. Davies explains, "...if there is any portion of the New Testament that is authentic, it is Paul's letter to the Galatians. If we cannot rely upon this letter, we can rely upon nothing and may as well close our inquiry. But the fact is that we can rely upon it. The letter to the Galatians is from Paul himself and by every test is genuine."[43]

---

[42] Ibid.
[43] A. Powell Davies, loc. cit., pp. 26-32.

THE FORMULATION OF THE GREEK GOSPELS

At this point let us consider the opposition of the Nazarene movement to the heresy of the Nicolaitans and, consequently, why the New Testament of the Gentiles has less in common with the Qumran Scrolls and *The Gospel of Barnabas* than the Scrolls and *The Gospel* have with each other.

Nazarenes' opposition to Nicolaitan Heresy

Whoever studies the New Testament becomes aware of the fact that it consciously portrays Paul as the perfect Apostle of the Apostolic Congregation (Nazarene Movement). No less than thirteen epistles in the New Testament are attributed to his authorship, but a large number of biblical scholars both Catholic and Protestant after years of research agree, that only seven of these are the authentic works of Paul. These are Romans; I and II Corinthians; Galatians; Philippians; Philemon, and I Thessalonians.[44]

Not only do the thirteen writings attributed to Paul comprise a quarter of the New Testament, but the larger part of the Acts of the Apostles, is also devoted to glorifying Paul, all in accordance with the general misrepresentation of him as a champion of the Nazarene reformation movement. But this impression of Paul's importance, both as leader and teacher in the Nazarene movement established by Jesus, and led in Jesus' absence by his brother James the Just, is by Paul's own testimony fictitious. Furthermore, this false impression given us about Paul's importance to the Nazarene movement is further dispelled by the internal evidence of Paul's own writings. When we read many of these works carefully, we sense an atmosphere of great tension. Paul often appears greatly concerned and agitated with what he considered to be the disturbing influence of certain

---

[44]Samuel Sandmel, op. cit., p. 309.

opponents, whom he will not name,[45] who preach among his own converts a gospel that differs from the Nicolaitan inspired doctrine he preached.

In our further analysis of the fictional nature of the doctrines propagated by Paul as opposed to the true Gospel preached by Jesus and his apostles, let us turn again to Paul's letter to the Galatians:

> But I make known to you, brethren, that the gospel which was preached by me is not according to man. For I neither received it from man, nor was I taught it, but it came through the revelation of Jesus Christ. For you have heard of my former conduct in Judaism, how I persecuted the church of God beyond measure, and tried to destroy it.
>
> And I advanced in Judaism beyond many of my contemporaries in my own nation, being more exceedingly zealous for the traditions of my fathers. But when it pleased God, who seperated me from my mother's womb and called me through His grace to reveal His Son in me, that I might preach Him among the Gentiles, I did not immediately confer with flesh and blood nor did I go up to Jerusalem to those who were apostles before me, but I went to Arabia, and returned again to Damascus. Then, after three years, I went up to Jerusalem to see Peter, and remained with him fifteen days. But I saw none of the other apostles except James, the Lord's brother. Now concerning the things which I write to you, indeed before God, I do not lie (Galatians 1:11-20).

If one reads this passage with a desire to understand what Paul is saying here, aside from his confession already discussed in the previous chapter, it becomes obvious that this passage provides us with three vital aspects of Paul's position as a teacher of Nicolaitan inspired doctrine. To defend this doctrine to his converts against the gospel preached by his opponents, Paul claims that he had not acquired it from any human source, and that in particular, he had not acquired it from the authentic apostles of Jesus, presiding at Jerusalem. Besides, this doctrine, as he claimed, had been revealed to him by God, through Jesus, for the specific purpose of revealing "His Son in me, that I might preach Him among the Gentiles." In other words, Paul claims that his Nicolaitan inspired teaching was specially designed to appeal to those who were not Jews. He, therefore, admits by implication that his doctrines differed from the authentic gospel preached

---

[45]Galatians, 1:6-9.

by the true apostles of Jesus. To convince his readers, he claims for them a divine origin.[46]

This is precisely the charge levelled against Paul by the Apostle Barnabas[47] in his introduction to *The Gospel of Barnabas*:

> True Gospel of Jesus, called Messiah, a new prophet sent by God to the world: according to the description of Barnabas his apostle.
>
> Barnabas, apostle of Jesus the Nazarene, called Messiah, to all them that dwell upon the earth desire peace and consolation.
>
> Dearly beloved, the great and wonderful God has during these past days visited us by His prophet Jesus (the) Messiah in great mercy of teaching and miracles, by reason whereof *many, being deceived of Satan, under pretence of piety, are preaching most impious doctrine, calling Jesus the Son of God*, repudiating the circumcision ordained of God forever, and permitting every unclean meat: among whom *also Paul* has been deceived, whereof I speak not without grief... I am writing that *truth* which I have *seen* and *heard,* in the fellowship that I have had with *Jesus,* in order that you may be saved, and not be deceived of Satan and perish in the judgement of God. Therefore, beware of everyone that preaches to you a new doctrine contrary to that which I write, that you may be saved eternally.
>
> The great God be with you and guard you from Satan and from every evil. Amen.

Obviously, within twenty years of the crucifixion incident the Nazarene movement of Jesus was faced with the challenge of subvertion from the Nicolaitans who were out to corrupt the Abrahamic faith by deifying Jesus and misrepresenting God as being nothing more than another pagan deity. As part of this conspiracy, Paul proclaims to the Galatians that his doctrine is designed to appeal to the Gentiles. The Apostle Barnabas has already identified those most noble opponents to the Nicolaitan heresy as being none other than himself and all the rest of the authentic apostles of Jesus. Paul gives us the same identification. In two seperate writings he refers to his noble opponents and the authentic gospel which they preached, in what Prof. Brandon calls "very remarkable terms." The first of these is the Galatian epistle, in which Paul writes in admonition to his converts:

---

[46]S.G.F. Brandon, op. cit., pp. 312-313.
[47]Acts 11: 22-24.

> I marvel that you are turning away so soon from Him who called you in the grace of Christ to a different gospel, which is not another; but there are some who trouble you, and want to pervert the gospel of Christ. But even if we, or an angel from heaven, preach any other gospel to you than what we have preached to you, let him be accursed. As we have said before, so now I say again, if any one preaches any other gospel to you than that you have received, let him be accursed (Galatians 1:6-9).

This attitude against the authentic apostles is also to be found in the Second Epistle to the Corinthians, which strongly implies that the apostles and their disciples were opposed to the propagation of Nicolaitan inspired doctrines at Corinth as well. Thus, Paul wrote in opposition to their activities:

> But I fear, lest somehow, as the serpent decieved Eve by his craftiness, so your minds may be corrupted from the simplicity that is in Christ. For if he who comes preaches another Jesus, whom we have not preached, or if you receive a different spirit, which you have not received, or a different gospel, which you have not accepted, you may well put up with it. For I consider that I am not at all inferior to the most eminent apostles. Even though I am untrained in speech, yet I am not in knowledge. But we have been thoroughly made manifest among you in all things (2 Corinthians 11:3-6).

"Paul's language in both passages," says Prof. Brandon, "is as amazing as it is significant. Paul does, in fact, witness to the currency in the Church of two rival interpretations of the faith. For the references to "another Jesus" and "a different gospel" must mean that Paul's opponents were teaching a different version of the meaning of the person and role of Jesus from that of Paul." Prof. Brandon goes on to ask who these opponents were, and then proceeds to point out that they could not have been some obscure sect of heretics, for if that were the case, Paul would surely have lambasted them with all that vehemence of speech of which he was so capable. "Clearly they were men who could operate so effectively within Paul's own missionfield," says Prof. Brandon, "as to cause him such concern." But Paul never explicitly names them or questions their authority. He does, however, give a clue to their identity in the passage just quoted, when he strikingly, adds after referring to this rival teaching, "...I consider that I am not at all inferior to the most eminent apostles." "There can be little doubt," writes Brandon, "in view of the facts just considered, as well as Paul's concern to assert his independence of the Jerusalem apostles, that those opponents who taught "another Jesus" were either the leaders of the Church in Jerusalem or their emissaries. In his epistle to the Galatians (2:1-10), when describing a later visit to Jerusalem, Paul gives details of these leaders. They formed a kind of triumvirate of what he calls *stuloi* ("pillars"); their names are James, Cephas (Peter) and John. The order in which these names are given is significant. James was clearly the leader; he precedes Cephas, i.e. Peter, etc."[48]

This opposition is also obvious from the following comparison of Paul's lawless teachings of his epistle to the Romans with the teachings in the epistle attributed to James the Just:

> But now the righteousness of God apart from the law is revealed, being witnessed by the law and the Prophets, even the righteousness of God which is through faith in Jesus Christ to all and on all who believe. For there is no difference; for all have sinned and fall short of the glory of God, being justified freely by His grace through the redemption that is in Christ Jesus, whom God set forth *to be* a propitiation by His blood, through faith, to demonstrate His righteousness, because in His forbearance God had passed over the sins that were previously committed, to demonstrate at the present time His righteousness, that He might be just and the justifier of the one who has faith in Jesus. Where is boasting then? It is excluded. By what law? Of works? No, but by the law of faith. Therefore we conclude that *a man is justified by faith apart from the deeds of law*. Or is He the God of the Jews only? Is He not also the God of the Gentiles? Yes, of the Gentiles also, since there is one God who will justify the circumcised by faith and uncircumcised through faith. Do we then make void the law through faith? Certainly not! On the contrary, we establish the law (Romans 3:21-31).

In his Nicolaitan inspired argument against the law of God, Paul drags the name of the Prophet Abraham into his attempt to belittle the law:

> What then shall we say that Abraham our father has found

---

[48] S.G.F. Brandon, op. cit., pp. 313-315.

78 *The Formulation of the Greek Gospels*

according to the flesh? For if Abraham was justified by works, he has something of which to boast, but not before God. For what does the scripture say? 'Abraham believed God, and it was accounted to him for righteousness.' Now to him who works, the wages are not counted as grace but as debt. But to him who does not work but believes on Him who justifies the ungodly, his faith is accounted for righteousness, just as David also describes the blessedness of the man to whom God imputes righteousness apart from works: 'Blessed are those whose lawless deeds are forgiven, and whose sins are covered; blessed is the man to whom the Lord shall not impute sin.'

Does this blessedness then come upon the circumcised only, or upon the uncircumcised also? For we say faith was accounted to Abraham for righteousness. How then was it accounted? While he was circumcised, or uncircumcised? Not while circumcised, but while uncircumcised. And he received the sign of circumcision a seal of the righteousness of the faith which he had while still uncircumcised, that he might be the father of all those who believe, though they are uncircumcised, that righteousness might be imputed to them also, and the father of circumcision to those who not only are of the circumcision, but who also walk in the steps of the faith which our father Abraham had while still uncircumcised (Romans 4:1-12).

In the epistle attributed to James, we find the following response:

Was not Abraham our father justified by works, when he offered Isaac his son on the altar? Do you see that faith was working together with his works, and by works faith was made perfect? And the scripture was fulfilled which says, 'Abraham believed God, and it was accounted to him for righteousness.' and he was called the friend of God. You see, then, that a man is justified by works, and not by faith only. Likewise, was not Rahab the harlot also justified by works when she received the messengers and sent them out another way? For as the body without the spirit is dead, so faith without works is dead also (James 2:21-26).

Although the Greek gospel of Matthew conceives of Jesus' return and his judgment of the Gentile nations in Greek concepts, yet it ironically gives support to James' emphasis on deeds (chapter 25) when Jesus is reported to have said that "... the righteous (will go) into eternal life."

The Spurious Nature of the Greek Gospels

The gospels of the New Testament, needless to say, are based in part upon the Nicolaitan misrepresentation of Jesus and his ministry, and in part upon elements derived from the authentic Gospel of Jesus. Thus, says Rev. Charles Anderson Scott:

> It is highly probable that not one of the Synoptic Gospels (Matthew, Mark, and Luke) was in existence in the form in which we have it, prior to the death of Paul. And were the documents to be taken in strict order of chronology, the Pauline Epistles would come before the Synoptic Gospels.[49]

In his work dealing with the religions of the world, Gerald L. Berry observes: "In addition to Paul's letters, the most important part of the New Testament is made up of the four Gospels. Although named after four of the disciples, they were not written by them." Berry continues, "No doubt a biography of Jesus in his own language, Aramaic, was written, and the Gospels were drawn from this, although the original is now lost. The Gospels were written in Greek a generation or two after Christ — the earliest one Mark, about the year 65, and the latest, John, about 100."[50]

But the authentic gospel of Jesus is not totally lost to us, for it is from a highly accurate gospel account compiled by Apostles Matthew and Barnabas, that we are now able to gain a relatively true account of the life and ministry of Jesus the Messiah.

The spurious nature of the Greek gospels is also confirmed by Prof. Brandon: "The earliest Christian writings that have been preserved to us are the letters of the Apostle Paul"[51] — a statement which clearly supports both Mr. Berry's and Rev. Dr. Scott's contention that the Greek gospels were not written by the real Matthew, Mark, Luke, or John. The practice of forging documents and falsely attributing them to other authors, such as the apostles, is well attested to in the early Gentile Church. Not only does Paul mention it (and remember out of all the epistles attributed to him in the New Testament, only seven are really his), but much later in the latter part of the second century we have the testimony of Dionysius Bishop of Corinth who says:

> As the brethren desired me to write epistles, I did so, and

---

[49] *History of Christianity in the Light of Modern Knowledge, A Collective Work*, op. cit., p. 338.
[50] S.G.F. Brandon, op. cit., p. 228.
[51] Ibid.

80 The Formulation of the Greek Gospels

> these the apostles of the devil have filled with tares (undesirable elements), exchanging some things and adding others, for whom there is a woe reserved. It is not, therefore, a matter of wonder if some have also attempted to adulterate the sacred writings of the Lord, since they have attempted the same in other works that are not to be compared with these.[52]

The spurious nature of the Greek gospels is further reflected in their inconsistency. When one who is unaware of the spuriousness of these documents turns to them, the first impression may well be that here we certainly have straightforward accounts of the life and ministry of Jesus. The impression, however, cannot be sustained when these spurious documents are carefully read and compared. Not not only is the misrepresentation of Jesus in the gospel of John distinctly different from that found in the other three Greek gospels, but the latter disagree among themselves on some fundamental points. For instance, the gospel of Matthew locates the appearance of the risen Jesus to the disciples in Galilee, where they are commanded to go (Matthew 28:7, 10, 16:20) — a story also found in Mark 16:7. The gospel of Luke and the Acts of the Apostles, both of which are attributed to the same author, locate the appearances of the risen Jesus in Jerusalem and its immediate vicinity (Luke 24:13-52; Acts 1:1-12). This is significant because Acts 1:4 clearly states that the apostles were forbidden to leave the city. "That such a discrepancy about so important a matter could exist," says Prof. Brandon, "surely indicates that the writings concerned embody traditions that must have grown up among different, and possibly rival groups of believers."[53]

That this is precisely the manner in which these forged gospels of the New Testament came about is admitted by Rev. Dr. Adam F. Findlay in a collective work on Christian history:

> None of the evangelic writings thus produced, not even those now in the New Testament, claimed on their appearance to have canonical authority; all alike were the offspring of the desire to present what was known or believed about Christ with the aim of satisfying the religious needs of the communities for which they were severally written. But as time went on, our four Gospels became widely known as the result of the constant intercourse which bound Christian

---

[52]Hugh J. Schonfield, *Those Incredible Christians*, Bantam Books, Inc., New York, 1969, pp. 135-137.

[53]S.G.F. Brandon, op. cit., p. 228.

communities together, and their pre-eminent value recognized by their use in public worship in the more important churches.[54]

Their usage in the more prominent churches and not their degree of authenticity caused them to be incorporated into the New Testament. In a book *All Scripture Is Inspired Of God And Beneficial,* it is admitted that there are nothing more than copies and copies of copies of earlier manuscripts in the possession of the Christian world, and that these copies, numbering 13,600, date no further back than the second to the fifteenth centuries. As a result of the Nicolaitan conspiracy, which did not stop with the death of Paul since he was not its founder, the Christians do not have the authentic Gospel of Jesus in their possession.

The spurious nature of these writings is not only reflected in the testimony of Bishop Dionysius, but also in the testimony of Victor Tununensis, a sixth-century African Bishop, who related in his Chronicle (AD 566) that when Messala was consul at Constantinople (AD 506), he *censored and corrected* the Gentile gospels written by persons considered illiterate by the the Emperor Anastasius. The implication is that they were altered to conform to sixth-century Christianity, which differed from the Christianity of earlier centuries. In response to this admission made by Bishop Tununensis, Sir Godfrey Higgins says: "As may be expected, great pains have been taken to run down and depreciate this piece of evidence to a dry fact, the truth or falsity of which the narrator must have known. Victor was a Christian Orthodox Bishop. It is not credible that he would in his Chronicle record a fact like this if it were false."[55]

The Ceaseless Corruption
Again in the eleventh and twelfth centuries, the Nicolaitan conspiracy to misrepresent the truth and thereby formulate a contrived universal religion resulted in further corruptions of already adulterated Christian documents. This time it was the joint efforts of Lanfranc, Archbishop of Canterbury, and Nicolas, Cardinal and Librarian of the Roman Catholic Church. As Sir Higgins says:

> It is impossible to deny that the Benedictine Monks of St. Maur, as far as Latin and Greek languages went, were a very learned and talented, as well as numerous body of men. In

---

[54]*History of Christianity in the Light of Modern Knowledge, A Collective Work,* op. cit., p. 318.
[55]Godfrey Higgins, op. cit., p. 682.

82 The Formulation of the Greek Gospels

Cleland's *life of Lanfranc, Archbishop of Canterbury,* is the following passage: 'Lanfranc, a Benedictine Monk, Archbishop of Canterbury, having found the Scriptures much corrupted by copyists, applied himself to correct them, as *also the writings of the fathers,* agreeably to the orthodox faith, secundum fidem orthodoxam.'

In other words, the Christian Scriptures were re-written once again so as to conform with the Nicolaitan inspired doctrines of the Christian religion as it was in the eleventh and twelfth centuries. "The same learned Protestant divine," says Sir Higgins, "has this remarkable passage (in his work): *'Impartiality exacts from me the confession, that the orthodox have in some places, altered the Gospels.'"*

Lanfranc was the head of the Monks of St. Maur about AD 1050, and it appears that this society not only corrupted the already corrupted spurious Gentile gospels further, but they also altered the writings of the early Church fathers, so that their alterations, which were made to conform them with the teachings of later-day Christianity, might not be discovered.[56]

During the age of Anastasius and Lanfranc the whole of the Christian world was under the control of the Emperor of Constantinople and the Pope, where religion was concerned. "I have no doubt," says Sir Higgins, "that there was a monastery, or priest of some sort, in every small district of Northern Africa, Egypt, Western Asia, and Europe. I cannot believe it possible that there should have been a hundred copies of the orthodox Gospels in existence which were not within the reach of the monks and priests, and I have no doubt that in either time, an order to correct the gospels given out at Constantinople, Rome, and Canterbury, would be competent to cause every copy, probably altogether not two thousand, to be rewritten. *This rationally accounts for the extraordinary fact of the destruction of all manuscripts before this period."*[57]

This attempt to destroy all of the manuscripts prior to this mass rewriting of Christian documents so as to make them conform to eleventh and twelfth-century Christianity further demonstrates the lengths to which the Church would go to hide the fallacy of its non-divine doctrines, and continue the manufacture of its man-made religion. It also implies that the kind of Gentile thinking that was involved in the original Nicolaitan conspiracy was still preeminent in the ongoing formulation of Christian

---

[56] Ibid.
[57] Ibid.

theology. Every student of Christian history knows that St. Augustine is looked up to by Catholics and Protestants alike as one of the early lights of their faith. He not only professed to teach that there were secret doctrines in the Christian religion, but he is said to have gone a step farther and to have affirmed *that there were many things true in the Christian religion which it was not convenient for the vulgar (lower ranks of the Church hierarchy and laymen) to know, and that some things were false, but convenient for the vulgar to believe in them.* As Sir Higgins points out:

> It is not unfair to suppose that in these withheld truths we have part of the *modern Christian mysteries*, and I think it will hardly be denied that the church, whose highest authorities held such doctrines, would not scruple to retouch the sacred writings."[58]

The result of the forged nature of the Gentile gospels from the beginning, their alteration in the fifth century, and re-alteration in the eleventh and twelfth centuries, is reflected in the inconsistency of their highly spurious accounts of the life and ministry of Jesus. In fact, their disagreement with each other is appalling. In a comparative study of the so-called gospel of John with the others, the so-called narrative of Jesus' life and ministry agrees with that of the other three in a few passages only. In an attempt to discover the degree of agreement between the gospels of Matthew, Mark and Luke, their texts have been divided into eighty-nine *imaginary* sections each; of these sections, forty-two are in general agreement, that is less than half. When Matthew and Mark are compared with each other, they have fifty-four sections in general agreement with each other, but the additional twelve sections held in common, differ with Luke. When Mark and Luke are compared with each other, they have only forty-seven sections in general agreement, but the additional five sections they have in common, having nothing in common with Matthew. When Matthew and Luke are compared with each other they have fifty-six sections in general agreement, but the additional fourteen sections common to both of them are not to be found in Mark.

It must be understood that what these spurious gospels of the New Testament do have in common is nothing more than general coincidences in the narratives (that is the stories told have some similarities). The amount of verbal coincidence, that is to say the passages that are either verbally the same or coinciding in the use of many of the same words is

---

[58]Ibid.

much smaller. Further comparison of the imaginary eighty-nine sections of the Gentile gospels falsely attributed to Matthew, Mark and Luke, brings to light that Matthew has five sections which do not appear in Mark or Luke. In turn, of its eighty-nine imaginary sections, Mark has two sections which do not appear in Matthew or luke, while Luke has nine sections out of its eighty-nine sections which do not appear in Matthew or Mark.[59]

The Gospel of John — A Gnostic Work

Of all these copies and copies of copies in the possession of the Christian world, the oldest of them is said to be the papyrus fragment of the so-called gospel of John, in the John Rylands Library in Manchester, England, known by the number P52. This fragment dates back to about AD 150.[60] The spurious nature of the gospel of John is obvious from the following statement made by the Biblical scholar Francis Crawford Burkitt:

> The contents of the Gospel of John do not seem to the present writer historical at all, in our sense of the word historical. Many of the incidents related in that Gospel are certainly based upon history, such as the Crucifixion itself, but they have all passed through the alembic (distillations) of the Evangelist's mind and have come out changed. I do not think the writer distinguished in his own consciousness between what he remembered (or had derived from the reminiscences of others) and what he felt must have been true, and I greatly doubt whether we can distinguish often in that Gospel what is derived from tradition and what is derived from imagination.[61]

On the same subject, in the same collective work on Christianity, the Rev. Dr. Charles Anderson Scott says: "The much debated question as to the authorship of the Gospel and the first Epistle of John has not yet been solved."[62] The importance of this admission can be seen in Edgar Hennecke's encyclopedic work: "The Roman church, it is true, at first exercised caution in relation to a Gospel which within its area stood in high favour with the heretics Ptolemaeus, Heracleon and Tatian. Here one either held one's peace as did Justin or allowed a presbyter Gaius, whose

---

[59] F.N. Peloubet, *Peloubet's Bible Dictionary*, Zondervan Publishing House Grand Rapids, MI., 1969, pp. 225-226.
[60] *All Scripture is Inspired of God and Beneficial*, Watchtower Bible and Tract Society of New York Inc., International Bible Students Associations, New York, 1963, p. 315.
[61] *History of Christianity in the Light of Modern Knowledge, A Collective Work*, op. cit., p. 209.
[62] Ibid., p. 383.

orthodoxy in its hostility to the heretics was beyond doubt, to dismiss not only the revelation but also the Fourth Gospel as forgeries of the Gnostic Cerinthus. Not until the beginning of the 3rd century does the opposition dwindle."[63]

The Gnostic nature of the gospel of John is unmistakable. According to the *Poimandres*, a notable Hermetic writing and a source for the pagan theology of the Gentiles, the pagan deity worshipped by the followers of this pagan system is portrayed as "Mind" (Greek nous) and the "Word" (Greek logos), which proceeded from the god as his son; in other words, the god as "Mind" emitted a living "thought" or "word" which became his son, and therefore the "son of god." This is precisely what we have in John 1:1-5.

In the theology of the fertility (agriculture) cult, the god is said to be incarnated as his own son to walk upon the earth in human form and be slain and ressurected as the personification of the harvest and plant life. Thus, in John 1:14, we read:"And the Word became flesh, and dwelt among us (and we beheld his glory, the glory as of the only begotten of the Father), full of grace and truth." Here the expression, "the Word was made flesh, and dwelt among us," is a Gnostic play on words so that the whole verse can be interpreted from a Gnostic point of view. Both man and animals are the words of God made flesh, since God has only to say "Be" and it is. From the Gnostic point of view the "Word" made flesh is a deity, an incarnation of their god. It is the misidentification of the "Word" as being one and the same with God, though at best it can only be a minute manifestation of His infinite power, that demonstrates the pagan nature of these verses in the gospel of John.

As stated elsewhere, Gnostics also drew upon the dualistic theology of the Persian Magi, and as every scholar and student of the subject knows, the Magian doctrines claimed that God (Ahura Mazda) had made Mithra the god of Truth and Light, a god equal in majesty to himself. Again, this is precisely what we have in John 1:6-14. The evidence implies that the Gnostic Cerinthus may very well have been the actual author of the gospel of John, just as the presbyter Gaius seems to have maintained all along. One thing is sure, the Apostle John had little or nothing to do with the formulation of this gospel. Whether it was Cerinthus or some other Gnostic, he was most likely a full-fledged member of the Nicolaitans and therefore deeply involved in their conspiracy, which formulated present-day Christianity.

---

[63]Willhelm Schmeemelcher, *New Testament Apocrypha, Vol. II,* The Westminister Press, Phila., PA, 1963, p.54.

IS THE GOSPEL OF BARNABAS THE ORIGINAL SOURCE?

In the first chapter of this work, we established the direct relationship between the Qumran Scrolls and *The Gospel of Barnabas* account of Jesus' life and ministry as documented by the Nazarene Apostle Barnabas. Let us now consider some additional evidence that further demonstrates the greater antiquity and authenticity of this gospel account. In so doing, we will further see the close relationship of the Nazarenes to the Essenic movement.

A primary example of the Nazarene and Essene relationship is the extensive usage of Essenic terminology in the Nazarene Gospel of Barnabas' as compared to the Hellenized (and later further corrupted) gospels of the New Testament. This indicates that Jesus and his apostles frequently used Essenic phraseology while explaining concepts to their people. Readers of the New Testament, *The Gospel of Barnabas* and the (Dead Sea) Qumran Scrolls who are familiar with this historical terminology will easily share our viewpoint.

For instance, the Essenic term, "holy one of God," appears thirty-six times in *The Gospel of Barnabas*, while this important term of spiritual endearment appears only twice in the Greek gospels (Luke 4:34 and Mark 1:24). Additionally, five variations of the same term appear in *The Gospel of Barnabas'* text, comprising another eight instances of its use.

As noted elsewhere, the Essenes also referred to, "the elect of God." This fundamental Essenic concept recurs in *The Gospel of Barnabas* twenty-three times. In contrast, the combined books of Matthew, Mark, and Luke make its reference merely seven times (Matthew 24:22, 24, 31; Mark 13:20, 22, 27; Luke 15:78).

"The poor ones," an Essenic self-description, may imply a possible connection with the "poor" spoken of in the Sermon on the Mount as it appears in *The Gospel of Barnabas*, and in a less accurate form in the New Testament. Furthermore, its Essenic usage indicates a connection with the Ebionites, who were also known as the "poor," and who may have been an Essenic sect.

Barnabas and the Compilation of The Gospel

Jewish sources concerning Jesus are unreliable. This may have come about because of Jesus' opposition to their corruption of the faith and compounded by the loss of accurate Judaic writings during the destruction of Jerusalem by the Romans in AD 70. Nonetheless, a surviving Jewish tradition indicates Jesus had five apostles, named Matthai, Naki, Nester, Bunni and Todah.[64] The number of apostles named notwithstanding, the name of Matthai remains significant. In the Christian document *Recognitions,* Matthias was another name for the Apostle Barnabas, and in another document known as *Homilies,* it is also stated that Barnabas was a personal apostle to Jesus, a strict servant of the Law, and therefore, one of the original twelve apostles. These references corroborate what we are told in *The Gospel of Barnabas* about him (Matthias):

> Jesus, having returned to the region of Jerusalem, was found again of the people with exceedingly great joy, and they implored him to abide with them, for his words were not as those of the scribes, but were with power; for they touched the heart.
>
> Jesus, seeing that great was the multitude of them that returned to their heart for to walk in the law of God, went up into the mountain, and abode all night in prayer. When the day came he descended from the mountain, and chose twelve, whom he called apostles, among whom is Judas, who was slain upon the cross. Their names are: Andrew and Peter his brother, fishermen; Barnabas, who wrote this, with Matthew the publican, who sat at the receipt of custom; John and James, son of Zebedee; Thaddaeus and Judas; Bartholomew and Philip; James, and Judas Iscariot the traitor. To these he always revealed the divine secrets. He made Iscariot Judas his dispenser of that which was given in alms, but he stole the tenth part of everything (*The Gospel Of Barnabas* 14).

What is said of Barnabas in *Homilies,* that he was a strict servant of the Law, is also said of Ananias: "And one Ananias, a devout man according to the law, having a good report of all the Jews who dwelt there." Ananias is also described as having been a disciple of Jesus the Messiah (Acts 9:10), which further proves that the Nazarenes, as the true followers of the Gospel of Jesus were genuine adherents of the Law to the best of their abilities.

---

[64]op. cit., p. 36.

Concerning the gospels of the New Testament and their lists of the apostles, even though the number twelve stands fast in these writings, the names and sequences vary to the point of disagreement between them. One of the apostles is called Lebbacus in (Matthew 10:13); Thaddaeus in (Mark 3:16:19) and Judas son of James in (Luke 6:16; and Acts 1:13).

The statement in *The Gospel of Barnabas* that "Barnabas, who wrote this, (the Gospel) with Matthew the publican, who sat at the receipt of custom," corresponds with what we are told in the Acts of Barnabas that Barnabas when going to Cyprus, took with him documents he had received from the Apostle Matthew "a book of the Word of God and a narrative of the miracles and doctrines." We are further told that in the synagogue at Salamis, the Apostle Barnabas unrolled the scrolls he had from Matthew, his fellow laborer, and began to teach the Jews there the authentic gospel of Jesus. The Church fathers of the early Christian Church agree that the Apostle Matthew compiled an account of the life and ministry of Jesus not in Greek, but in Hebrew. Papias (AD 144) stated in his work, now lost, that the Apostle Matthew compiled *Oracles* in the Hebrew language, and that each interpreted them as he was able.[65] It was from the scrolls written by Matthew and those in his own hand that Barnabas compiled his account of the Prophet Jesus, the Messiah of the Israelites, in the Hebrew tongue.

As to the precise time of its compilation, one can say that Barnabas must have decided to embark upon this project following his trip to Cyprus with Paul when the latter had his crucial encounter with Bar-jesus, and went astray.

Paul's Decision to Become a Nicolaitan

From the account in Acts, which glosses over the fact that Paul began to oppose the authentic Gospel of Jesus the Messiah while on this journey, we may be able to glean the truth concerning the events leading up to Paul's decision to join the Nicolaitans. At whatever point in his life he may have been rejected by the family of the High Priest of the Jews and prohibited from marrying his daughter, Paul does not seem to have rebelled against the Jews and the Mosaic Law until after this journey in which he met Bar-jesus the sorcerer and Sergius Paulus the Roman official. The conversion story and all of the other Nicolaitan inspired fabrications Paul is guilty of appears to have come about after this encounter. Prior to this meeting with Sergius Paulus and Bar-jesus, he may have been genuinely interested in the Nazarene movement founded by Jesus. If he sought some vengeance

---

[65]Eusebius Bishop of Caesarea, *Ecclesiastical History*, Book 111, 11 & 39, trans. C.F.Cruse, Bell & Sons, London, 1874, p. 39.

against the Jewish High Priest and his family, he may have thought that the Nazarenes would be of help to him in this endeavor, since they may have appeared to him to be anti-Jewish — in the religious sense — and therefore against the Law. Thus, his visit to Peter's home, and so on. The fact is, the Nazarenes were for the Law of God and against the corruption of the Law, of which the Jews were guilty.

As said before, Jesus' mission was to restore the Abrahamic faith among the Jews and thereby restore the fallen house of Israel. But more than this, his mission was to bear to his people the glad tidings of he who was yet to come. This expectation the Nazarenes held in common with other Essenic sects. When Paul realized that the Nazarenes would not serve his purpose of getting back at the Jews, as the Nicolaitan sect of Gnostics would, he switched and joined them in their conspiracy against the Israelite children of Abraham, their God, His Law, and therefore the Abrahamic religion.

According to the account in Acts, when Stephen was stoned after his trial by the Jewish Sanhedrin (Council) his accusers, who were obligated by Jewish law to cast the first stones, laid down their garments and did so (Acts 7:58-60). "And there arose on that day," so the story goes, "a great persecution against the (community, for there was no church in the present sense) that was in Jerusalem, and they were all scattered abroad throughout the regions of Judea and Samaria, except the Apostles (Acts 8:1). "As for Saul, he made havoc of the church entering every house and dragging off men and women, committing them to prison" (Acts 8:3).

As to the dispersal of the persecuted ones, Acts says: "Now those who were scattered after the persecution that arose over Stephen traveled as far as Phoenicia, Cyprus, and Antioch, preaching the word to none but the Jews only. But some of them were men from Cyprus and Cyrene who, when they had come to Antioch, spoke to the Hellenists (6:1), preaching the Lord Jesus" (Acts 11:19-20).

It is obvious that Stephen, who is identified as a Hellenized Jew, was stoned for blasphemy. The composer of Acts identifies Stephen and his Hellenized Jewish followers as Nazarenes, but the identification is inaccurate, for the persecution of these Hellenized Jews did not include the Nazarenes whose political position, like other Essenes was anti-Hellenistic. That they were not dispersed abroad is evident from the fact that Nazarene leaders such as Peter and John, far from disparaging the Temple admittedly visited it every day. Though it cannot be discounted that such leaders as Peter and John may have been brought before the Sanhedrin and told to stop preaching their reformation message, they were never charged with blasphemy. Only Stephen, his Hellenized Jews, and Paul (Saul) ran into such difficulty, which makes the obvious, obvious.

Because of the environment in which they were born and raised, many

Hellenized Jews were susceptible to the idea of Jesus being a god. Stephen and his followers were no exception. They sought to preach this pagan notion promoted by the Roman soldiery. Obviously, they were persecuted for their blasphemous lies and antinomian tendencies, while the Nazarenes who were also opposed to this blasphemous belief were not. This is also why, when word reached the Apostolic governing body of the Nazarene movement at Jerusalem that some of Stephen's followers were in Antioch preaching their blasphemous doctrines, it quickly dispatched the Apostle Barnabas, perhaps with some assistants, to Antioch to counteract the propaganda (Acts 11:22). "For he, Barnabas, was a righteous man" — "a man of faith." His efforts paid off — many people joined the Nazarene movement to restore the Abrahamic religion among the Israelites and prepare for the coming of the expected one.

Now, because Paul was apparently passing himself off as a Hellenized Jew, and because he appeared to be sincerely dedicated to the cause and showed potential for perseverance and an ability to teach, Barnabas either departed for Tarsus to seek him out, or he sent for him. The composer of Acts thought it would be more effective to have Barnabas go himself, or have Saul (Paul) come to Antioch on his own and be accepted by Barnabas as an assistant. The latter is more plausible. At any rate, they came together at this time. We know from the introduction to *The Gospel of Barnabas* that Barnabas had a sincere fondness for Paul. Based on the book of Acts, it appears that they worked together for a whole year assembling a body of believers in the authentic Gospel of Jesus (Acts 11:22-26).

In the Nazarene community at Antioch, there were certain people, including the Apostle Barnabas, who were gifted with spiritual insight and were good teachers. Aside from Barnabas, persons gifted were Symeon, who was called Niger (because he was of Alke-bulani African descent), Lucius of Cyrene, and Manaean, who had been brought up with Herod, the tetrach. Saul (Paul) was also part of this community. It came to pass that Barnabas was dispatched from Antioch, either by virtue of James' message brought to him by John Mark, or by virtue of a visionary dream, or by his own decision. The possibility of his cousin Mark bringing him such a message cannot be discounted because John Mark's presence is not mentioned during Barnabas' stay at Antioch. He is thrust into the reader's consciousness only after the journey had begun (Acts 13:1-5).

No matter what the actual route of the journey may have been, they eventually went to Paphos where they encountered the Hellenized Jewish sorcerer and false prophet Bar-jesus (son of Jesus), who was also called Elymas. The sorcerer was an associate of the Roman proconsul Sergius

Paulus, whom we are told sent for Barnabas and Paul in order to have them explain the teachings of Jesus to him. But the sorcerer sought to withstand them and prevented the proconsul from becoming a believer, or both the sorcerer and the proconsul were working together to try and persuade both Barnabas and Saul as well as Mark to become Nicolaitans as the sorcerer appears to have been (13:6-8). The author of Acts sought to conceal the fact that it was Barnabas and not Saul (Paul) who withstood the sorcerer by the power of God. But the truth which he apparently overlooked is right there in his narrative in verse 9, of the thirteenth chapter where the name change from Saul to Paul suddenly takes place. For if Paul's statement in Acts 22:28, can be believed, then he was "free born," which means that his father was a Roman citizen, and as such extended citizenship to his son Paul upon his birth. This means that the name change in verse 9 has nothing to do with his acquisition of citizenship. It also supports — as circumstantial evidence — the charges leveled against him by the Ebionites.

Evidence suggests that Paul came across the Nicolaitan, Bar-jesus, and whoever might have been with him as a fellow sectarian, which may have included Sergius Paulus, and having embraced their heathen doctrines changed from a Nazarene, or one professing to be, to a Nicolaitan. The change perhaps did not come overnight, but over a brief period of time. This may well be what the composer of Acts is conveying, though he would most likely have viewed it as nothing more than a break with the mission to the circumcised, unless he himself was a Nicolaitan. It was during his period of brooding over having been rejected by the High Priest that Paul realized — if the Ebionites were right — that the Nicolaitan conspiracy would best serve his purpose. Further evidence in support of this supposition is provided by the following verse where the composer of Acts replaces Barnabas the legitimate leader of the missionary team of Barnabas and company, with Paul and company:

> Now when Paul and his party set sail from Paphos, they came to Perga in Pamphylia; and John, departing from them, returned to Jerusalem (Acts 13:13).

The reason for which John Mark left the missionary team must have been to inform the apostolic governing body at Jerusalem that the Nicolaitans have succeeded in causing Paul to deviate from the true way. The association of Barnabas and Paul from this point on (Acts 13:14-52 through 15:1-35) is supplied by the author of Acts from his fertile imagination to convince the average reader that Paul was still on excellent terms with Barnabas. Whether an intelligent reader will accept such a travesty of facts, the author of Acts are not concerned with. They hope though that the average Gentile reader will believe that the doctrines preached by Paul were acceptable to the Nazarenes.

But insidious as this manuever was, as early as the latter part of the first century (when Acts was written), it had become evident that Paul had turned away from the Antiochian orthodoxy. In other words, he had gone astray from the true Gospel preached by the authentic apostles such as Barnabas and others at Antioch and elsewhere. The Nicolaitans and their followers believed that if they could succeed in giving the impression that Barnabas was still Paul's companion after the latter went astray, then the charges against him could be dismissed as untrue. But the pretense could not be continued even in the highly imaginative work known as Acts. The final phase of the split between Barnabas and Paul, and consequently Paul's split with the Nazarenes following John Mark's return to Antioch, was dealt with in such a way as to gloss over the facts. Thus we read the following:

> Then after some days, Paul said to Barnabas, 'let us now go back and visit our brethren in every city where we have preached the word of the Lord, and see how they are doing.' Now Barnabas was determined to take with them John called Mark. But Paul insisted that they should not take with them the one who had departed from them in Pamphylia, and had not gone with them to work. Then the contention became *so sharp* between them that they *parted* from one another. And so Barnabas took Mark, and sailed to Cyprus (Acts 15:36-39).

All of the evidence presented so far makes it clear that Barnabas wrote his gospel, using his own compilations and those of Matthew, to counteract the Nicolaitan conspiracy after his break with Paul.[66]

Further Evidence Concerning the Great Antiquity of The Gospel of Barnabas

As a result of decades of careful study of the spurious documents in the New Testament, biblical scholars, not blinded by the traditional Nicolaitan inspired propaganda, became somewhat aware that behind these spurious gospel histories resided a legitimate statement concerning Jesus. However, they contend, based on the limited evidence at hand and perhaps

---

[66]A. Powell Davies, op. cit., pp. 42-43.

because of some personal prejudices, that only so-called gospels of Matthew and Luke are derived from a common source, which they refer to as "Q" (from the German Quelle, meaning source). But if we assign the name "Q" to the gospel account of Jesus by Barnabas and Matthew (as is proper based upon the evidence), then we have correctly identified the legitimate source of those fragments of truth here and there throughout the New Testament.[67]

Now out of the ignorance of the historical facts concerning the gospel account compiled by the Apostles Barnabas and Matthew, Christians like Pantaenus, when confronted by a copy of this work, erroneously thought that it was the sole work of the Apostle Matthew. Thus, we find it stated in a book on ecclesiastical history that Pantaenus, an eminent Egyptian Christian who lived in the late second century, while visiting the East, "...found the Gospel of Matthew, which had been delivered before his coming to some who had knowledge of Christ, to whom Bartholomew, one of the apostles, as it is said, had preached and left them that writing of Matthew in Hebrew characters." Pantaenus, according to Jerome, took this copy back with him to Alexandria. The misconception that the Apostle Matthew was the sole compiler of the authentic gospel history of Jesus is also found in the *Acts of Barnabas*, for it states that upon the martyrdom of Barnabas, the manuscripts in his possession were secretly placed in a cave with his remains.

According to early Christian historians, when the relics of the Apostle Barnabas were discovered in Cyprus in the fourth year of the Emperor Zeno (AD 478), there was found lying on his breast a copy of the gospel of the Apostle Matthew written by his own hand.[68] Thus, we see how the gospel compiled through the joint efforts of Matthew and Barnabas was taken as the sole work of Matthew. There was never any question of accuracy or authenticity, for this was a quarter of a century prior to the mass alteration of the early Gentile gospels in the sixth century. Thanks to such alterations, the Nicolaitan inspired doctrines of the Church became fully entrenched in the Christian world.

The Jewish Rebellion, the Anti-Semitism of the Gentiles and the Survival of The Gospel of Barnabas

Events within the Christian Church leading up to the sixth-century form of Christianity sheds some light on why the Church would reject the authentic teachings of Jesus and the gospel history of the apostles Barnabas

---

[67] *History of Christianity in the Light of Modern Knowledge, A Collective Work*, op. cit., p. 210.
[68] Bolland: Junii, tom, *Acta Sanctorum, pp. 422 sgg. and 450 (Antwerp, 1968)*.

and Matthew. But before we consider these events, we must first understand how the Greeks of the Apostolic period, famous for their strong anti-Jewish feelings, were able to establish a Church openly hostile to the Jewish people, their religion and culture.

First of all, Jewish resistance to the heathen kingdom of Rome had been in evidence long before the public teaching of Jesus. But with the death of the Jewish king Agrippa I in AD 44, and the intensification of the oppressive policies of the Roman procurators, the Jewish frustration reached a new high. It was agreed by the righteous in Israel that heathen Rome with its Graeco-Roman culture dedicated to the glorification of immorality, brutality, injustice, and all the gods was the arch-enemy of the one true God and His people. It was identified with the Fourth Kingdom, the worst of all predators of the prophecy in Daniel: 7.

In their naivety, the Jews thought that the time for the fullfilment of the prophecy had come, forgetting that their Scriptures had been corrupted by the impious among them. Filled with messianic zeal, they rose in rebellion against imperial Rome at a time when they had no chance of winning. Recounting the event, Josephus the Jewish historian wrote: "What more than all else incited them (the Jews) to the war was an ambiguous oracle, likewise found in their sacred scriptures, to the effect that at that time one from their country would become the ruler of the world. This they understood to mean someone of their own race, and many of their wise men went astray in their interpretation of it." Although the oracle is not specified, Josephus may be referring to Numbers 24:17-18. *The Targum of Onkelos* here paraphrases the passage, "When a king shall arise out of Jacob, and the Messiah shall be anointed from Israel, he will slay the princes of Moab, and reign over the children of men; and Edom (Rome) shall be an inheritance."[69]

With messianic fervor urging them on, the struggle with Rome was a terrible one in which guerila tactics and burning patriotism all played a part. The tragic outcome was reached when the destruction of Jerusalem and the Temple occurred in AD 70.

The loss of life in the rebellion was appalling. Josephus estimated that one million one hundred thousand lost their lives in the Roman seige of Jerusalem alone. Prior to this, many thousand are believed to have died or been killed in Jerusalem and in other parts of the country. The number of prisoners taken by the Romans throughout the rebellion was ninety-seven thousand. Of the people who survived the seige, the freedom fighters, the

---

[69]Trans. William Whiston, *Life and Work of Flavius Josephus,* John C & Winston Co., Chicago, p. 825, and Hugh J. Schonfield, *The Passover Plot,* Bantam Books Inc., New York, 1969, pp. 184-185.

feeble and the elderly were slaughtered. Eleven thousand prisoners perished from starvation before the Roman authorities could make up their minds what to do with them, and the death toll continued to mount with those who were sent to the mines, or to the various provinces to be killed in the theaters by the sword or wild animals.

Although Graeco-Roman Gentiles would later have the audacity to profess to be the spiritual heirs and propagators of the Abrahamic religion in accordance with spurious gospel histories composed by their own hands, their anti-Jewish stance is reflected in the historical fact that at the beginning of the Jewish revolt against Rome, the Gentile citizenry of Casarea massacred the Jews living in their city. Within an hour's time they murdered more than twenty thousand people; and as a consequence, Casarea was completely emptied of Jews, for all survivors were arrested by order of Florus and taken in chains to the dockyards. Upon reaching Lydda, Gallus found the town deserted, because its inhabitants had gone to Jerusalem. Upon his discovery of fifty persons who had remained behind, he set about slaughtering them and setting a torch to the town.[70]

In Galilee, where Jesus had lived and spent much of his time preaching, and where the resistance was deeply rooted, the Romans carried on their slaughter of the inhabitants night and day. They devastated the plains and plundered the property of the country-folk, invariably slaughtering all who might bear arms against them and reducing those left to slavery. "Galilee from end to end became a scene of devastation. From no misery, no calamity was it exempt." The Romans also slaughtered a great number of Galileans along the shore of Lake Galilee. The whole lake was red with the blood of the slaughtered and covered with corpses, for not a man escaped. For days the area reeked with the stench of rotting bodies."[71]

The Nazarenes, as we have seen, had their headquarters at Jerusalem. It was there that James the Just, Jesus' brother, had presided with the aid of the original apostles over the affairs of the movement until his judicial murder in AD 62. The Nazarenes in AD 66, knowing the truth about the messianic prophecies, refused to join the rebel forces against Rome holding the belief that the heathen should be left to God's vengeance. In accordance with "the command of an oracle," the Nazarenes in body abandoned the doomed city of Jerusalem and took flight eastward across the Jordan into the Arabian territory of Jordan called Decapolis at the time, toward a city called Pella. The subsequent fall of Jerusalem in AD 70 was a partial fulfillment of Jesus' prophecy recorded in *The Gospel of Barnabas*, and the spurious gopels attributed to Matthew, Mark, and Luke in the New

---

[70]Ibid., pp. 699-700.
[71]Ibid., pp. 714-715, 766.

Testament.[72]

Concerning the survivors of the war with Rome, early rabbinical literature talks about the large-scale Jewish suffering and the chaotic period preceding it. Many, particularly members of the older generation, were seriously impaired in health and memory. People who might have been capable of providing testimony of importance on past events, including information about the life and ministry of Jesus, made contradictory statements, got dates mixed up, and person and events confused, which might well be a contributing factor to the unreliability of the Jewish traditions concerning Jesus and the Nazarenes. Nevertheless, despite the devastation, hardships and loss of memory, the gospel history compiled by the Apostle Barnabas (Matthias) survived because it rested undisturbed upon the apostle's breast until discovered in AD 478. Other copies were probably made from this work for Nazarene usage prior to Barnabas' demise, which survived the Nazarene flight into Pella. This is reflected in the historical account given to us concerning Pantaenus' discovery of a copy in the "East," which he brought back with him to Alexandria.

The Establishment of the Christian Church and the Nicolaitan Conspiracy

Another consequence of the devastation heaped upon the inhabitants of Palestine and the Jewish people living elsewhere was the difficulty and eventual termination of guidance and communication from the Apostolic body in the East with the Nazarene congregations in the West. It is this unfortunate state of affairs within the Nazarene movement that led to the official establishment of the Christian Church by the Nicolaitans and those influenced by them to teach false doctrines. Doubtless, the early history of the Christian Church is intertwined with the history of the Gnostic movement, which aimed at establishing a universal syncretic religion composed of pagan elements. On the rise of Gnosticism, Rev. Charles Harold Dodd says, perhaps without fully realizing its implications:

> Out of this ferment of religious speculation arose a kind of vague theosophy, highly characteristic of the age in which Christianity began. It aimed at being a universal religion comprehending within its hospitable creed all partial faiths. Its God was a transcendent Absolute, communicating with the

---

[72]Luke 21:5-6; Trans. William Whiston, op. cit., p.598; Hugh J. Schonfield, *The Passover Plot* op.cit., p.186.

98   Is The Gospel of Barnabas the Original Source?

world through a hierarchy of intermediate intelligences, in which it was possible to recognize the gods of the popular cults.

On the same subject he writes:

Already about AD 100, the fourth Gospel presents salvation, or eternal life, in the guise of knowledge of God, attained through His self-revelation in the Logos (John 17:3; 1:18 and so on) and the affinities of its teachings with those of Philo and of pagan thinkers such as the Hermetic writers are unmistakable. (The Church Father) Clement of Alexandria expressly claims the name of Gnostic for the enlightened Christian.[73]

In AD 64, there was a community at Rome which professed to be part of the Nazarenes. This community appears to have been nearly wiped out by the Romans, who are said to have put the majority of them to death on the pretense that they had set the great fire in which a considerable portion of Rome was destroyed, while Nero is said to have played his lyre. Any increase in converts to this community following this tragic episode was offset once more at the hands of the Gentiles as a result of the Jewish rebellion against Rome. The majority of those persons professing to be Nazarenes who had survived these two catastrophes were largely Gentiles, susceptible to the cunning tactics of indoctrination employed by the Nicolaitans.

The noted scholar William Smith says that the great controversy concerning obedience to the Law of God was inevitable as soon as the Gentiles were allowed to enter the Nazarene movement in large numbers. Taken along with the notorious anti-Semitism of the Greeks, it strongly suggests the presence of Nicolaitans in the Roman congregation following the fall of Jerusalem in AD 70.

The same must have been true to varying degrees in the other western congregations due to their significant Gentile membership. The general history of these congregations after the fall of Jerusalem in AD 70 bears this out. In fact, the Greek presence in the congregation at Rome is also verified by William Smith, who explains in his Bible dictionary that the captives taken to Rome by Pompius formed the core of the Jewish population there. He goes on to say: "On the other hand, situated in the metropolis of the

---

[73]*History in Christianity in the Light of Modern Knowledge, A Collective Work*, op. cit., pp. 434-436.

great empire of heathendom, the Roman Church must necessarily have been in great measure a Gentile Church; and the language of the Epistles bears out this supposition." He says further: "These Gentile converts, however, were not for the most part native Romans. Strange as the paradox appears, nothing is more certain than that the Church of Rome was at this time a Greek and not a Latin Church."[74] Thus, all of the literature of the early Roman Church, especially the New Testament, was written in Greek, not because any of the authentic apostles could possibly speak Greek, but because the Gentile Church from which sixth-century Christianity sprang was a Greek institution. Consequently, the bishops of Rome during the first two centuries were but for few exceptions, Greek. And thus we find that a very large proportion of the names in the salutations of Paul's epistle to the Romans are Greek.[75]

Notwithstanding the success of the preaching campaign carried out by the Nazarenes against Paul and the rest of the Nicolaitans, the Nazarenes flight to Pella and the fall of Jerusalem left a vacuum, which encouraged the Nicolaitans to continue their relentless attack upon the upholders of the Abrahamic faith. Deprived of communication and guidance from the apostolic body in the East as a result of the post-war chaotic conditions, the western congregations came to believe — with or without the instigation of the Nicolaitans — that the apostolic body of believers was dead or scattered, and that they had to fend for themselves as best they could. Seizing upon the situation, the Nicolaitans in the western congregations and the Christian Church which emerged under the circumstances decided to condemn the Jewish and Nazarenes' opposition to Roman impiety and dominance. For the Gnostic movement to succeed in establishing a universal cult based upon a conglomeration of pagan beliefs, the Roman authorities had to be appeased. Steps in this direction were taken by substituting the Abrahamic religion with the pro-Roman doctrine preached by Paul. (Romans 13:1-7). Indeed, the very existence of Christianity as a universal system of belief bears witness to the success of the Nicolaitans in this endeavor. This success is fully in accordance with the prophecy spoken by Jesus:

> ...there shall come a great number of false prophets, whereas I sorrow. For Satan shall raise them up by the just judgement of God, *and they shall hide themselves under the pretext of my gospel!* Herod answered, 'How is it the just judgement of God

---

[74] William Smith, op. cit. Articles: Nicolaitans, p. 450, and Epistle to the Romans, p. 580.
[75] Ibid, p. 580.

that such impious men should come?' Jesus answered, 'It is just that he who will not believe in the truth to his salvation should believe in a lie to his damnation. Therefore, I say to you that the world has always despised the true prophets and loved the false, as can be seen in the time of Michaiah and Jeremiah. For every like loves his like (*The Gospel of Barnabas* 97).

Gradually, through an ongoing of propaganda, Pauline theology was accepted by the western congregations. This occurred through the cunning ploys of the Nicolaitans, even though it had been rejected by the eastern as well as many western congregations because of the Nazarene's successful campaign against the Nicolaitans. To disguise the break with the authentic Gospel of Jesus, the Nicolaitans altered the epistle written by James the Just to the various congregations to make it a transitional piece of literature between the authentic Gospel preached by Jesus, his apostles and the rest of the true believers, and the spurious gospel promoted by the Nicolaitans. The very first verse of the Epistle of James shows the corrupting handiwork of the Nicolaitans within the Church where Jesus is equated with God. Other obvious instances of corruption in its text are 1:25 (i.e., law of liberty instead of Mosaic law), 2:1 (i.e., the Lord of Glory is a Gnostic term); 2:8-12 (the insinuation that he who stumbles in one point is guilty of all — that it is only through grace one can be saved); 3:9; 5:11 (i.e., coming of the Lord is a substitution for the coming of the expected one); and 5:14-16 (i.e., the use of the title Lord interchangably for Jesus and God). Along with this manuever was their promotion of the epistles actually written by Paul, and the Epistle to the Hebrews falsely attributed to Paul. It did not take Paul to become the hero of the western congregations. Copies of Paul's epistles were widely circulated and studied, and in time collected together they formed the literature of what was developing into the Christian Church. That is why the Scillitan Christians (executed at Carthage in AD 180), when asked about the literature in their possession, replied that they possessed "ancient books of divine laws (Greek version of the Old Testament) and the letters of Paul a just man."[76]

A further step in this Nicolaitan engineered transition from the Nazarene movement to Christianity was the fabrication of the mythical tale that the Apostle Peter was the founder of the Greek congregation at Rome. We are told in the notable work done by William Smith that "the origins of the Roman Church is involved in obscurity," and "if it had been founded by St.

---

[76]Hugh J. Schonfield, op. cit., pp. 129-132.

Peter, according to a later tradition, the absence of any allusion to him both in this Epistle (Romans) and in letters written by St. Paul from Rome would admit of no explanation. It is equally clear that no other Apostle was the founder." As to Christianity having reached Rome during the life of Jesus, Smith says: "The statement in Clemintines that the first tidings of the Gospel reached Rome during the lifetime of our Lord is evidently a fiction for the purpose of the romance."[77] Along with this fiction went the misrepresentation of Peter as the chief apostle of the Nazarene movement, when in fact it was James the Just, the brother of Jesus, who was chosen to succeed Jesus. This was fully in accordance with the Nazarene practice, for we find that after the war it were the members of Jesus' family who were chosen to lead the Nazarene movement.

Such were the events which led to the emergence of the Christian Church at Rome. With its predominant Gentile membership, it had an innate anti-Semitic attitude, which surfaced violently at the sight of any document that would expose the fallacy of the Christian religion, particularly if it had been written or compiled by a Nazarene or a Jewish Israelite. Consequently, during the reign of the Christian Emperor Flavius Theodosius (AD 379-395), all writings that were not in conformity with the doctrines of the Roman Christianity were burned, with the approval of the Emperor and the Church. Again, during the reign of the Christian Emperor Valentinian III (AD 425-454), the emperor issued an order to burn all writings opposed to the Roman version of Christianity. In this manner, it was hoped that the truth would never be revealed. With this policy of suppression, the Nicolaitan instituted Church compiled an index of prohibited books known as the *Decretium Gelansium*. On the whole, this index is probably of South Gallic origin (6th century), but at a number of places it has been traced back to Pope Damasus (336-384) and reflects Roman tradition. Needless to say, this index *inter alia* prohibits the authentic gospel history written by the Apostles Matthew and Barnabas under the title *Evangelium Barnabae*. The manner in which this benevolent gospel survived all attempts to suppress and destroy such work is tied to the history of the Nazarene after the Jewish war of rebellion against Rome, for only they would have had an interest in preserving its existence. Unfortunately, much of their history has been lost to us. We do know they survived as an independent religious body in the Middle East up to the fifth century, which brings us to the topic of the next chapter.

---

[77]William Smith, op. cit., p. 580.

THE PROPHET WHO WAS TO COME

After the death of Jesus and the destruction of Jerusalem in AD 70, the Nazarene movement had to be rebuilt. With the majority of adherents scattered throughout the East and the Nicolaitan conspiracy dominating western congregations, the issue of new leadership emerged as a critical one for the Nazarenes.

Writing on the subject, the historian Eusebius says that those apostles and disciples of Jesus who survived, together with members of his family, met to settle the issue of succession. They decided upon first cousin Simeon, son of Cleophas, who lived to the advanced age of 120 before his martyrdom. Cleophas had been a brother of Joseph, the father of Jesus. Also associated with the approved leadership of the movement at that time were James and Sokker, the grandsons of Jesus' brother Jude.

Meanwhile, Roman fear of a resurgence of Jewish nationalism inspired by the messianic prophecies caused the Emperor Vespasian to order all descendants of David arrested, so that no one belonging to the ancient Jewish royal family would be left free to foment rebellion. Despite their harrasment at the hands of the Roman authorities, the family of Jesus and the rest of the Nazarenes established a governing body of their religious movement.[78]

In their search for the true Abrahamic religion and messianic prophecies, a large number of Jews joined the Nazarene Congregation. Accurate rabbinical sources also attest to the success of the true Gospel of Jesus among the Jewish people after the war. This prompted the Roman authorities to kill Simeon who was a descendant of David and a Nazarene. At the time the Romans barely knew the difference between the true believers in Jesus' Gospel and the misguided souls, known as Christians who believed in the Nicolaitan inspired doctrines of the Church.

---

[78]Eusebius Bishop of Caesarea, op. cit. Book III, 11, & 39.

Nevertheless, they soon realized that those known as Christians were very much like themselves in their beliefs.

Upon Simeon's death the succession of leadership passed to an Israelite named Justus, who was not one of the heirs *(desposyni)*, for so the family of Jesus was known. Justus, in turn, was succeeded by twelve other Israelites whose names were preserved down to AD 132. According to Eusebius, all of these successors to the leadership of the Nazarene movement were Hebrews and received the knowledge of Jesus the Messiah pure and unadulterated, a clear admission that the Christians had developed a corrupted version of the Gospel.

Conflicting Messianic Prophecies at the time of Jesus
A further parallel of great interest and immense importance is the Essene and Nazarene belief in the advent of two messiahs. The Nazarenes recognized Jesus as having been the messiah who came, and in accordance with Jesus' prophecies, they looked forward to the advent of the messiah who was yet to come. In the Essenic work known as the *Manual of Discipline* (9:8-11), there is a confusing reference to the expected advent of the messiahs. It talks of three apostles of God instead of just two:

> Until the coming of the Prophet and both the priestly and the lay messiahs, these men are not to depart from the clear intent of the law to walk in any way in the stubborness of their own hearts. They shall judge by the original laws in which the community was schooled from the beginning.

As a result of the Jewish corruption of the Scriptures, one can perceive what appears to be a multitude of expected messiahs in Jewish writings. According to the messianic expectations of the Jews during the general time period in which Jesus appeared, the son of David was the most popular messianic concept among the people. This concept of the messiah was based upon Psalms 17 and 18, Zechariah and Malachi, and the second part of Isaiah (which is the spurious part of that book, as explained in an earlier chapter). This concept of a pastoral king who would be a monarch in the temporal sense, ruling the same territory over which David had once ruled, was also based upon the Sibyline Oracles and the Psalter of Solomon. This messiah would be born of a young mother in Judean Bethlehem — the Bethlehem of Ephrath — after many wars, famines, and natural calamities, at a time when the Jews would be floundering in a sea of misery. This prophesied period was refferred to as "the pangs of the Messiah." This messiah was to be summoned from an obscure home and anointed king by the *ever-young* Elijah. Elijah was to prepare the way for this Messiah, who would thereupon enter Jerusalem riding in triumph on a young ass. This would be the signal for a bloody war against Jerusalem by the oppressors of Israel, in the course of which the city of Jerusalem would be taken and two-thirds of the inhabitants massacred. This Messiah, however, encouraged by divinely inspired omens, would rally the faithful survivors on the Mount of Olives and lead them to final victory. He would then re-unite the scattered tribes of Israel and reign peacefully for four hundred years or, some said, a thousand years, with the rulers of Egypt and Assyria and the rest of the world paying homage to his throne in the newly sanctified city of Jerusalem. This kingdom of Heaven would be an era of great prosperity, a new Golden Age.

Another prophecy foretelling messiahs who were to come was of "The Son of Ephraim," a warrior messiah, whose birthplace would also be Judean Bethlehem. His reign was to be primarily over the ten Israelite tribes of the North which had seceded from Rehoboam, the last king of the united monarchy of Israel. Since it was held by the Jews that the town of Shechem had been defiled by the presence of its Samaritans, it was thought by some that this prophesied Messiah would return to Shechem and cleanse it. Other Jews thought that his appearance would instead occur on Mount Tabor, the holy mountain of Galilee.

The "Son of Ephraim" (also known as the Son of Joseph) was, in fact, a rival concept of the messiah(s) to that of the "Son of David" concept. Many of the Galileans held that the blessings conferred by Jacob (Israel) on his sons (Genesis 49:10), did not justify Judah's claim to the perpetual leadership of Israel. When this prophecy is fulfilled, they claimed, the royal sceptre and the commander's baton would be handed over by Judah to the Messiah. This Messiah they further said must be a Josephite, since Jacob had prophesied that from Joseph would spring forth the Shepherd, the Rock of Israel, and that blessings were in store for him "to the utmost limits of the everlasting hills." This conception of the messiah was associated with a preacher of repentance, who might be Elijah.

Another concept of the messiah(s) that was held by some of the Jews, was "The Son of Man." This concept was based upon an interpretation of Daniel 7, where a certain "Son of Man" is given everlasting dominion by the Ancient of Days over all nations. The whole concept, as presented in Daniel, is mystical and not literal. The term "Son of Man" is nothing more than another way of saying "man", "human being," "homo sapien." Thus, in the book of the Prophet Ezekiel, the Prophet Ezekiel is repeatedly referred to as the "son of man."

Still another concept of the Jews concerning the messiah(s) who was to come was a priest-king supported by a Judean general. This concept was based on the Testament of Levi. As a priestly Messiah, this person must necessarily come from the tribe of Levi. This concept of the messiah involved the sanctification of the generals' conquests and the establishment of universal peace, reformation of the calendar, revision of the Scriptural Canon, and the cleansing of the Hebrew people from their sins.

And then there was the concept of "The Warrior Messiah," confused with "The Son of David" concept by some, and with "The Son of Ephraim" (or "Son of Joseph") by others. It was believed by the upholders of this tradition that, according to Isaiah, he would come marching out of Edom which, in Isaiah's day, lay outside Israelite territory. It was said that he would wear dyed garments from Bozrah. At that time, the city of Bozrah on the Persian Gulf was the site of a centuries-old purple dyeing industry. The Edomite capital was also called Bozrah.[79]

With so many confused traditions concerning the advent of the messiahs, it is no wonder that so many Jews even now fail to recognize Jesus as their Messiah, and the one who was to come after Jesus. However, as previously pointed out, following the war of rebellion a large number of Jews joined the still active Nazarene movement. Thus, the Rabbinic sources roughly correspond with the gospel account of Matthew and Barnabas, that a great multitude of Jews recognized Jesus as one of their great prophets. The evidence implies that following the calamities of the Jewish war of rebellion against the Romans, a large number of these Jews came to look upon these calamities as the foretold "pangs of the Messiah," and Jesus as having been their Messiah.

In the Essenic work known as the *Zadokite Document*, the Essenic expectation of the two messiahs is presented in clearer language than in the statement from the *Manual of Discipline* quoted earlier. The *Zadokite Document* says:

> And these, in specific form, are the regulations which they

---

[79]Robert Graves and Joshua Podro, op. cit., pp. 14-15.

are to follow throughout the Era of Wickedness, until the priestly and lay 'messiahs' enter upon their office expiate and expiates their iniquities (Zadokite Document 14:18).

In *The Gospel of Barnabas*, we find the same theme of two messiahs. Jesus is presented as having been the Messiah who was the predecessor of the Messiah who was yet to come:

> The woman answered, 'We look for the Messiah; when he comes he will teach us.'
> Jesus asked, 'Do you know woman that the Messiah must come?
> She answered, 'Yes, Sir.'
> Then Jesus rejoiced and said, 'So far as I see, O woman, you are faithful. Know therefore that in the faith of the Messiah shall be saved every one that is elect of God. Therefore, it is necessary that you know the coming of the Messiah.'...
> Jesus answered, 'I am indeed sent to the house of Israel as a prophet of salvation, but after me shall come the Messiah, sent of God to all the world, for whom God has made the world. And then through all the world will God be worshipped, and mercy received, insomuch as that the year of Jubilees which now comes every hundred years shall by the Messiah be reduced to every year in every place.'
> Then the woman left her waterpot and ran to the city to announce all that she had heard from Jesus (*The Gospel of Barnabas 82*).

The basic Essenic theme of two messiahs is stated many times in *The Gospel of Barnabas* in the light of prophecies made by Jesus concerning that theme. Another presentation of that theme is as follows:

> Jesus answered, 'There are written in the prophets many parables; thus, you ought not to attend to the letter, but to the sense. For all the prophets, which number one hundred and forty-four thousand, whom God has sent into the world have spoken darkly. But after me shall come the splendor of all the prophets and holy ones, and he shall shed light upon the darkness of all that the prophets have said, because he is the messenger of God (*The Gospel of Barnabas 17*).

The Harassment of the Nazarenes and Jesus' Prophecy about the Coming Messiah

Notwithstanding the harassment by the Roman government, the family of Jesus carried on their propagation of the Gospel of Jesus to restore the Abrahamic faith among the Israelites. Their negation of the corrupted form of the faith practiced by others and their opposition to the Jewish desire to placate the Roman government made the Nazarene a menace in the sight of the rabbins. Consequently, the rabbinists from about AD 90 sought to exclude the Nazarenes, the Essenes in general, and all upholders of the concept of the Last Day and messianic enthusiasm from the synagogues. At the same time, the Nazarenes were opposed and eventually despised by the Christian Church, which had arisen through the agency of the Nicolaitans from its former congregations in the West. The western congregations, which formed the Christian Church, rejected the very Gospel of Jesus.

Oppressed and afflicted from all sides, and thus forced to live for the most part in outlying areas of Galilee, Aurantis and Gaulantis, the Nazarenes carried on the work of propagating the Gospel of Jesus, making numerous converts while taking heart in the knowledge that they were right, for Jesus had prophesied that this situation would befall the teachers of truth:

> Believe me, because I tell you the truth, that the world will greatly fear you if you shall observe my words. For if it feared not to have its wickedness revealed it would not hate you, but it fears that it will be revealed; therefore, it will hate you and persecute you. If you see your words scorned by the world take it not to heart, but consider that God, who is greater than you is also scorned by the world that His wisdom is counted madness. If God endures the world with patience, will you take it to heart, O dust and clay of the earth? In your patience you shall possess your soul (*The Gospel of Barnabas 18*).

The Nazarenes suffered especially during the period of persecution initiated by the Emperor Domitian, and later in the Jewish revolt under the messianic pretender, Bar-Cochba (Koziba) when they refused to recognize his messianic claims. Jesus' prophecies concerning the Messiah did not permit the Nazarenes to mistake Bar-Cochba for the Messiah who was still to come:

> When the prayer was ended, the priest said with a loud voice: 'Stay, Jesus, for we need to know who you are, for the quieting of our nation.'

Jesus answered, 'I am Jesus, son of Mary, of the seed of David, a man who is mortal and fears God, and I seek that God be given honour and glory.'

The priest answered, 'In the book of Moses it is written that our God must send us the Messiah, who shall come to announce to us that which God willed, and shall bring to the world His mercy. Therefore, I pray tell us the truth, are you the Messiah of God whom we expect?'

Jesus answered, 'It is true that God has so promised, but indeed I am not he, for he was made before me, and shall come after me.'

The priest answered, 'By your words and signs at any rate we believe you to be a prophet and a holy one of God. I pray in the name of all Judea and Israel that you, for love of God, should tell us how the Messiah will come.'

Jesus answered, 'As God lives, in whose presence my soul stands, I am not the Messiah whom all the tribes of the earth expect, even as God promised to our father Abraham saying: "In your seed will I bless all the tribes of the earth." But when God shall take me away from the world, Satan will raise again this accursed sedition, by making the impious believe that I am God and the Son of God. At such time, my words and my doctrine shall be contaminated so much that scarcely shall there remain thirty faithful ones. At that time, God will have mercy upon the world and will send His messenger for whom He has made all things. He shall come from the south with power, and shall destroy the idols and the idolaters. He shall take away the dominion which Satan has over men. He shall bring with him the mercy of God for salvation of those who shall believe in him, and blessed is he who shall believe his words' (*The Gospel of Barnabas* 96).

The Messiah that Jesus Spoke of

In the late second century, as the *Memoirs of Hegesippus* says, a man was found collecting traditions about the life and ministry of Jesus from the Nazarenes and Christians in order to write a general ecclesiastical history. Whatever was the nature of such an ecclesiastical history, one thing can be said for sure that the traditions carried prophecies about the Messiah who was to come after Jesus. So pervasive was their presence in the eccelesiastical literature that even the Nicolaitans Church of Rome retained them, though in a distorted form.

The Gospel of Barnabas is, however, clear on the subject. In a very poignant scene, Barnabas recounts to his readers the conversation between Jesus and his disciples on the issue:

> Then the disciples wept after this discourse, and Jesus was also weeping, when they saw many who came to find him, for the chiefs of the priests took counsel among themselves to catch him in his talk. They sent the Levites and some of the scribes to question him, saying, 'Who are you?'
> Jesus confessed and said the truth, 'I am not the Messiah.'
> They said, 'Are you Elijah or Jeremiah, or any of the ancient prophets?'
> Jesus answered, 'No.'
> Then said they, 'Who are you? Say, in order that we may give testimony to those who sent us.'
> Then said Jesus, 'I am a voice that cries through all Judea, and cries, "Prepare you the way for the messenger of the Lord," even as it is written in Esaias.'
> They said, 'If you are not the Messiah or Elijah, or any prophet, why do you preach new doctrine, and make yourself more important than the Messiah?'
> Jesus answered, 'The miracles which God work by my hands show that I speak that which God wills; nor indeed do I make myself to be accounted as him of whom you speak. For I am not worthy to loosen the shoe straps of the messenger of God whom you call "Messiah," who was made before me, and shall come after me, and shall bring the words of truth, so that his faith shall have no end.'
> The Levites and scribes departed in confusion, and recounted all to the chiefs of the priests, who said, 'He has the devil on his back who recounted all to him' (*The Gospel of Barnabas 42*).

Now compare John 1:19-27 with the preceding passage from *The Gospel of Barnabas*. It is obvious how the Gnostic author of the gospel of John distorted the passage to hide the truth.

In Sir Godfrey Higgins' notable work *Anacalypsis*, we are told that in the *Book of Haggi*, the name of the Messiah who was to come after Jesus appears in chapter two, verse seven: "And the desire of all nations shall come." Here the Hebrew letters HMD, from the Hebrew text appears in Sir Higgins' work with the following explanation of the root word HMD. "From this root," (says Parkhurst,) "*the pretended prophet Mohammed, or Mahomet,* had his name." Sir Higgins says, "Here Mohammed" is expressly foretold by Haggi, and by name; there is no interpolation here. There is no evading this clear text and its meaning, as it appeared to the mind of the most unwilling of witnesses, Parkhurst, and a competent judge too when he happened not to be warped by prejudice. He does not suppress his opinion here, as he did in the case of the *Wisdom of the Jerusalem Targum*, because he had no object to serve; he did not see to what this truth would lead."[80]

A Messiah from the Ishmaelites

We need not be surprised that the messiah who was yet to come was an Ishmaelite. The Bible's insistence upon the racial, political and economic relations with Arabia is a definite indication of Israel's spiritual and cultural inheritance being rooted in Arabia. Because of this and the important role the Ishmaelite people have played for the Abrahamic religion, Israel had its face turned toward those quarters we call the Desert. By God's design this was its nearest neighbor. The Ishmaelites are the first cousins to the Israelites, and the eldest of Abraham's offspring. Therefore, the Ishmaelites and the true Israelites are more closely related to each other than to the other branches of the Semitic cultural groups. They are, both obligated by virtue of the Abrahamic Covenant with God to refrain from worshipping false gods:

> And I will establish my covenant between me and thee and thy seed after thee in their generations for an everlasting covenant, to be a God unto thee and to thy seed after thee (Genesis 17:1).
> And the Lord said, Shall I hide from Abraham that thing which I do;
> Seeing that Abraham shall become a great and mighty nation, and all the nations of the earth shall be blessed in him?
> For I know him, that he will command his children and his household after him, and they shall keep the way of the Lord, to do righteousness and justice; that the Lord may bring upon Abraham that which he hath spoken of him (Genesis 18:17-19).

After all it was Ishmael (he whom the Lord God will hear), who was the first of Abraham's offspring to enter into the Abrahamic Covenant with God (Genesis 17:23-26), to worship no other god but God (Genesis 17:6-8). Therefore, when the Ishmaelites strayed from the Abrahamic faith like

---

[80]Godfrey Higgins, op. cit., p. 679.

their brethren the Israelites, they too were entitled to a prophet like Moses to facilitate their return to the Abrahamic religion of their forefathers. This is because of their blood affinity and their being parties to the Covenant that when Jehu, founder of the fifth dynasty of Israel, revolted against the growing idolatry in Israel during his lifetime (II Kings 10:14), the Rechabite Arabs did not hesitate to join him as willing allies against idolatry (II Kings 10:15-28).

Furthermore, because the Ishmaelites and Israelites were adherents of the same religion, with minor differences due in part to different historical experiences, their socio - religious formation had more in common with each other than with their surrounding neighbors. The evidence of the Old Testament, even in its present form, clearly points to Arabia as the crucible in which the Supreme Fashioner by design, through a series of circumstances, molded the Ishmaelite and Israelite nations. These elements plus divine revelation provide us with the finished product, the divine religion of Abraham. Obviously, we must honor the tradition of the Abrahamic religion expressed in the Book of Ezekiel that it came by way of the Arabian desert: "And behold, the glory of the God of Israel came from the way of the east; and His voice was like a noise of many waters, and the earth shined with his glory" (Ezekiel 43:2). The "east" here refers to Arabia, for as demonstrated by William Smith and others who have compiled Bible dictionaries, the term "east country" (Genesis 25:6), and "land of the sons of the east" (Genesis 29:1) refers to Arabia.

Finally, let us consider the fact that among a number of Arab tribes the name Yahweh (Jehovah) was used for God. Searching for the etymological origin of this name for God, Prof. Theophile J. Meek discovered that the name Yahweh was foreign to the Isrelites, and that in fact it is of Arabian origin. This is in accord with the Old Testament records, which connect the name with the Arabian tribes of the Negeb and with southern sanctuaries like Sinai-Horeb and Kadesh. The research further indicates that the most probable origin of the name "Yahweh" for God, is from the Arabic root *hwy*, "to blow."[81] Prof. William F. Albright has also traced the name "Yahweh" back to its Arabic root *hwy*, the full significance of which, is: "He who causes what is to come into existence."[82] Consequently, it is not surprising to find that the Arab father-in-law of Moses, the prophet and lawgiver of God, was not only an Arab sheikh, but a priest (Heb. kohen) of Yahweh (God), "who was a man of sound judgement": "For forty years Moses communed with God and with nature, and enjoyed intimate

---

[81]Joseph Campbell, *The Masks of God: Accidental Mythology*, Penguin Books, New York, 1976, p. 132.
[82]William F. Albright, *From The Stone Age to Christianity*, 1957, pp. 15-16.

association with Jethro, a man of sound judgement" (Exodus 18). It was his father-in-law, Jethro the priest and therefore a worshipper of Yahweh (God), who instructed Moses in the Abrahamic religion.[83]

The evidence clearly demonstrates that the prophecy of an Arabian prophet, as being the messiah who was yet to come, was perfectly in accordance with the Abrahamic inheritance and tradition. And history certainly has demonstrated the accuracy of the prophecy.

From the Book of Haggi alone, Jesus and the rest of the Nazarenes could have discovered the knowledge of the name of the prophet and messiah who was yet to come. Being a prophet of God, Jesus must have received such knowledge through divine revelation. In *The Gospel of Barnabas*, we also find the name of the Messiah who was to come after Jesus:

> 'Verily I say to you that every prophet when he comes is borne to one nation only the mark of the mercy of God. And so their words were not extended save to that people to which they were sent. As for the messenger of God, when he shall come, God shall give to him as it were the seal of his hand, so much so that he shall carry salvation and mercy to all the nations of the world that shall receive his doctrine. He shall come with power upon the ungodly, and shall destroy idolatry, so much so that he shall make Satan confounded, for so promised God to Abraham, saying: "Behold, in your seed I will bless all the tribes of the earth; and as you have broken in pieces the idols, O Abraham, even so shall your seed do."
>
> James answered, 'O master, tell us in whom this promise was made; for the Jews say "in Isaac," and the Ishmaelites say "Ishmael."
>
> Jesus answered, 'David, whose son was he, and of what lineage?'
>
> James answered, 'Of Isaac, for Isaac was father of Jacob, and Jacob was father of Judah, of whose lineage is David.'
>
> Then asked Jesus, 'And the messenger of God when he shall come, of what lineage will he be?'
>
> The disciples answerd, 'Of David.'
>
> Whereupon Jesus said, 'You deceive yourselves, for David in spirit called him lord, saying thus, "God said to my lord, sit at my right hand until I make your enemies your footstool. God

---

[83]Philip K. Hitti, op. cit., p. 40.

shall send forth your rod which shall have lordship in the midst of your enemies." If the messenger of God whom you call Messiah were the son of David, how would David call him lord? Believe me, for verily I say to you that the promise was made in Ishmael, not in Isaac' (*The Gospel of Barnabas 43*).

Thereupon said the disciples, 'O master, it is thus written in the book of Moses, that in Isaac was the promise made.'

Jesus answered with a groan, 'It is so written, but Moses wrote it not, nor Joshua, but rather our rabbins, who fear not God. Verily, I say to you that if you consider the words of the angel Gabriel, you shall discover the malice of our scribes and doctors. For the angel said: 'Abraham, all the world shall know how God loves you, but how shall the world know the love that you bear to God? Assuredly it is necessary that you do something for the love of God.' Abraham answered, 'Behold the servant of God, ready to do all that which God shall will.'

'Then spoke God, saying to Abraham, 'Take your son, your firstborn Ishmael, and come up the mountain to sacrifice him.' How is Isaac firstborn, if when Isaac was born Ishmael was seven years old?'

Then answered Jesus, 'Verily I say to you that Satan ever seeks to annul the laws of God. Therefore he with his followers, hypocrites and evildoers, the former with false doctrine, the latter with lewd living, today have contaminated almost all things, so that scarcely is the truth found. Woe to the hypocrites, for the praises of this world shall turn for them into insults and torments in hell.

'I therefore say to you that the messenger of God is a splendor that shall give gladness to nearly all that God has made, for he is adorned with the spirit of understanding and of counsel, the spirit of wisdom and might, the spirit of fear and love (of God), the spirit of prudence and temperance. He is adorned with the spirit of charity and mercy, the spirit of justice and piety, the spirit of gentleness and patience, which he has received from God three times more than He has given to all his creatures. O blessed time, when he shall come to the world. Believe me that I have seen him and have done him reverence, even as every prophet has seen him. Seeing that of his spirit God gives to them prophecy. And when I saw him my soul was filled with consolation, saying, "O Muhammed, God be with you, and may he make me worthy to untie your shoe laces, for obtaining this I shall be a great prophet and holy one of God.'

And having said this, Jesus rendered his thanks to God (*The Gospel of Barnabas 44*).

Evidence from Beyond Israel

Prior to, and perhaps as early as the first century AD, a segment of the Nazarene movement seem to have migrated across Persia into Kashmir and South Asia. That they passed through Persia is evident from the following excerpt from the Parsi Scripture — the glad tidings (Gospel) brought by Jesus to the Israelite people:

> When the Persians would sink so low in morality, a man will be born in Arabia whose followers will upset their throne, religion and everything. The mighty stiff-necked ones of Persia will be overpowered. The house (of God) which was built (in Arabia) and in which many idols have been placed will be purged of idols, and people will say their prayers facing towards it. His followers will capture the towns of Parsis and Taus and Balkh and other big places round about. People will embroil with one another. The wise men of Persia and others will join his followers (Dassatir 14).

In chapter ninety-six of *The Gospel of Barnabas* Jesus speaks of the Messiah who was to come after him as coming "from the south (of Palestine) with power, and shall destroy the idols with the idolaters." Any good Bible dictionary will point out the fact that the Arabians inhabited the lands to the east and south of Palestine.[84]

Evidence of the Nazarenes' entry into Kashmir is obvious from the traditions of local people. They describe a tomb that belongs to an immigrant who bore the Kashmiri name Yuz Asaf and was known as a great teacher. It is said that Yuz Asaf came to Kashmir from western Asia 2000 years ago. A historical work known as *Tarikh A'azami*, written over a century ago and drawing upon ancient Kashmiri traditions, also speaks of Yuz Asaf, as does the *Ikmal ad-Din*, an Arabic work, which was written nine centuries earlier than *Tarikh A'azami*. It informs us that Yuz Asaf had traveled in some lands prior to reaching Kashmir. According to a very old version of this tradition, Yuz Asaf's name is rendered Juasaph or Joseph, which clearly identifies him as having been a Hebrew. The fact that he identified his teachings as being the Gospel (Arabic, Bushra) reinforces the evidence that he was one of the disciples of Jesus.

---

[84] F.N. Peloubet, op. cit., p. 42.

One of the ancient traditions concerning the Nazarenes speaks of them as a wandering tribe of Abhiras of the first century AD, who are said to have migrated from Syria or Asia Minor into South Asia, and brought with them traditions concerning the birth of Jesus the Messiah, the massacre of the innocents, and so on. The Hindi name "Abhira" as applied to this particular group of Nazarenes was probably derived from their national name in Hebrew, "Ibhri," which means "Hebrew." Their identification with non-Hebrew tribes of South Asia bearing the name Abhira was probably because both groups were wandering herdsmen. Further indication of the Nazarene presence in South Asia prior to AD 189, is reflected in the Christian account of Pantaenus of Alexandria who was sent to South Asia in AD 189 by Demetrius Bishop of Alexandria, reportedly at the request of a congregation there. Unless it was another attempt by the Nazarenes to show the Christians the error of their ways and doctrines, here out of the reach of the Roman authorities and Christian Church, Pantaenus found a flourishing Nazarene community which the account alleges was founded by the Apostle Bartholomew. This community of Nazarenes were, by error or design, misidentified as Christians in the account. In their possession was a copy or copies of the gospel account compiled by the Apostles Matthias (Barnabas) and Matthew, which was in use among them. A copy of that Pantaenus took back to Alexandria with him, probably as proof that the Nicolaitans inspired doctrines of the Church were erroneous. After all, the western congregations that now formed Christiandom had once been part of the Nazorean movement, and the Nazarenes must have still cared for them as a mother does for her wayward child.

Hiding the Truth
Behind the double Meaning

It was a practice common to pagans, though not exclusively theirs, to use the double meaning of words to convey certain ideas or messages. But whereas teachers of truth used metaphors to teach certain truths, pagans often used metaphors to hide the truth, such as the fact that they were worshippers of men. Thus Alexander of Macedonia, who is called by some, "the Great," wrote to his mother: "Even the higher gods, Jupiter, Juno and Saturn and the other gods *were men,* and that the secret was told to him by Leo, the high priest of Egyptian sacred things." He went on to instruct his mother to burn the letter, obviously to keep the secret from the layman.[85] On the same subject, Col. Garnier says, "Everything with them had an

---

[85] Col. J. Garnier, op. cit., p. 15.

"exoteric" or outward meaning, and an 'esoteric' or inward meaning. The Sun was exoterically the supposed source of natural life, but esoterically it represented the source of spiritual life."[86]

In an analysis of the New Testament, we find that there are esoteric (hidden) references to the Messiah who was to come after Jesus. These references are more distinguishable in the Greek than in the English text. Here we will consider the key words in Greek and then consider their meanings to see how the truth has been hidden:

> And I will pray the *Patera*, and he shall give you another *Paraclete*, that he may abide with you forever;
> Even the *pneuma* of *alethia*, whom the world cannot receive, because it neither sees him nor knows Him: but you know him, for he dwells with you, and will be in you (John 14:16-17).

The esoteric (hidden) meaning:
> And I will request that the Nourisher (Sustainer = God) send you another Messenger, so that he may be (your guide) always,
> The inspired, the Truthful, whom the world at large will not welcome because it will not comprehend or appreciate him, but you (who believe) will recognize him. He will dwell with you and (his message) will find a place in your hearts.

The standard English is designed to hide the facts even more so than the Greek documents from which they were derived:

> And I will pray the Father, and He will give you another Comforter, that he may abide with you forever.
> Even the Spirit of Truth, whom the world cannot receive, because it neither sees Him nor knows Him; but you know Him, for He dwells with you, and will be in you.

"...He will give you another Comforter." Here Jesus is made to identify himself as a Comforter, and to identify the Messiah who was to come after him as a Comforter when, in fact, they were both Messengers of God. But even the exoteric term, "Comforter" in the place of "Messenger" does not fully hide the facts, for of Noah the prophet of God, it is said: "And Lamech lived an hundred eighty and two years, and begot a son. And he called him Noah, saying, 'This same shall *comfort* us concerning our work and toil of our hands...'" (Genesis 5:28-29). Now as one may know, a person who

---

[86]Ibid, p. 216.

gives comfort is a Comforter. So whether they have Jesus identify the Messiah who was yet to come as a Comforter or Messenger, the significance is the same: it is a reference to the Prophet of Arabia who came after him.

The repeated reference to Muhammed as the "Spirit of Truth" by the author, or authors of the gospel falsely attributed to John the son of Zebedee, is quite in accordance with the Gnostic method of interpretation. The following prophecy concerning Muhammed in *The Gospel of Barnabas* greatly influenced the composer of the so-called gospel of John:

> He (Muhammed) shall come with truth more clear than that of all the prophets, and shall reprove him who uses the world amiss (*The Gospel of Barnabas* 72).

Again in John 15:26, and 16:13, we find the Prophet Muhammed referred to as the "Spirit of Truth." In Luke 24:49, the prophecy is not presented in language as clear as the verses previously quoted, while John 14:26, is an obvious attempt to be more mystical in the exoteric expression of the esoteric fact that there was a prophet, a Messiah as the Jews called him, who was to come after Jesus. Indeed, history substantiates this fact. The Greek term "Paraclete" which means "Messenger" as well as "Comforter," as pointed out, was utilized by the Gentiles to replace the original term "Periclyte," which means "Illustrious," which is another meaning of the Messenger's name, "Muhammed." John 14:16-17, in its original form, essentially stated the following: "And I will request that our Nourisher (Sustainer = God) send you the Illustrious One (Ar. Muhammed) so that he may be your guide always, the Inspired, the Truthful (Ar. al-Amin) whom the world, and so on."

George Sale admits in his "Preliminary Discourse to the Qur'an" that the term Peryclyte in Arabic means illustrious, which is the meaning of the name Muhammed.[87] It also carries the meaning praiseworthy. Says Sir Higgins: " Bishop Marsh has observed that this word Paraclete must have been the Syraic or Arabic word prqlit (Peryclyte) translated into Greek." He goes on to say: "Now I maintain that if, as Bishop Marsh says, the word *prqlit* was the word used by Jesus, and that it means illustrious, it is a gross

---

[87] Godfrey Higgins, op. cit., p. 679.

See also, Sanders and Mastin, *The Gospel According to St. John*, p. 83, for the significance of the Greek term alethia as corresponding to the Arabic term 'Amin — truthful, and also Rudolph Bultmanns, *The Gospel of John*, p. 567, for the definition of Paraclete as messenger.

mistranslation to render it by (Paraclete) which means comforter."[88]

Further substantiation of our stance that the hidden mysteries of the early Gentile Church are preserved in esoteric form (certain truths not convenient for the vulgar to know, as St. Augustine is said to have put it) is obvious from the following historical account related by Mr sale in his preface "To the Reader" of his edition of the Qur'an:

> ...the discoverer of the original M.S., who was a Christian monk called Fra Marino, tells us that having accidentally met with a writing of Irenaeus (among others), wherein Irenaeus spoke against Paul, alleging, for his authority, the Gospel of St. Barnabas, he became exceeding desireous of finding an existing copy of this Gospel, and that God of His mercy, having made Fra Marino an intimate friend of Pope Sixtus V, (pope, 1585-1590), one day, as they were together in the Pope's library, his Holiness fell asleep, and the monk, to occupy himself, reaching down for a book to read, the first he laid his hand on proved to be the very Gospel history that he was seeking. Overjoyed at the discovery, he scrupled not to hide his prize discovery in his sleeve; and, on the Pope's awakening, took leave of him carrying with him that celestial treasure, by reading of which he became a convert to Muhammedanism."

Now in light of all the evidence including the Pope's possession of the Gospel of St. Barnabas, the implication is that at least some members of the upper hierarchy of the Gentile Church as late as the sixteenth century were in possession of the truth concerning the messianic prophecies uttered by Jesus to his apostles. This now brings us to a most interesting but little known episode in Christian history related by the English writer, Sir Higgins. As every learned person on the subject knows, the early Gentile Church claimed spiritual descent from the Apostle Peter, whom it presented as being the chief apostle of the original twelve authentic apostles. But as William Smith in his Dictionary points out about the church at Rome: "If it had been founded by St. Peter, according to a later tradition, the absence of any allusion to him both in his Epistle (Romans) and in the letters written by St. Paul from Rome would admit of no explanation. It is equally clear that no other Apostle was the founder. The statement in the Clementines that the first tidings of the Gospel reached Rome during the lifetime of our Lord is evidently a fiction for the purpose

---

[88]Ibid.

of the romance."[89] In accordance with this fiction, promoted in an attempt to give an air of legitimacy to the Nicolaitan established Christian Church, the office of Pope, as the spiritual descendant of Peter, also claimed that it held the key of heaven, and the power to grant or refuse absolution for sins, to open or close the gates of heaven. "This is evidently a grand step to universal empire," says Sir Higgins, "and it is not surprising that great exertions should have been made to establish it." He goes on to point out that various miracles have been attributed by the early Gentile Church to the Apostle Peter, which it claimed took place at Rome, and that in order to further support the credit attributed by it to the Apostle, the chair alleged to be of the Apostle Peter, was formerly exhibited by the Church. Since Peter was regarded as holy, it followed that the chair he sat upon was also holy. A festival for the holy chair was, therefore, instituted by the Church on the 18th of January. Every year on that day the chair was exposed to the adoration of the people. This practice by the Church was continued down to the year AD 1662, when upon cleaning it, the labors of Hercules appeared engraved on it beneath the accumulated soil.

"Our worship," says Giacomo Bartolini, who was present when the discovery was made, "however was not misplaced, since it was not the wood we paid it, but to the prince of the apostles, St. Peter." Commenting on the subject Higgins says: "An author of no mean character unwilling to give up the holy chair, even after this discovery, as having a place, and a peculiar solemnity among the other saints, has attempted to explain the labours of Hercules in a mystical sense, as emblems representing the future exploits of the Popes"..."But the ridiculous and distorted conceits of that writer," observes Higgins, "are not worthy of our notice, though by Pope Clement X, they were judged not unworthy of a reward."

When the French gained possession of Rome, they examined the celebrated chair of the Apostle Peter, and to their astonishment, in addition to the labors of Hercules, they discovered that engraved on the chair, in the Arabic tongue, was the Muslim confession of faith: "There is no god but God," and in its fullest sense is the addition of the statement: "and Muhammed is the Apostle of God."[90] Now behind the presence of this chair in Italy, in the early seat of Christian power, decorated with the twelve labors of Hercules and the Muslim confession of faith, Sir Higgins perceived a mystery. The chair was brought to the Vatican from Constantinople by a Christian pilgrim, and it was a matter of wonder to Sir Higgins how the Church officials could not have been aware of the

---

[89] William Smith, op. cit., p. 580.
[90] Godfrey Higgins, op. cit., pp. 691-694.

emblems and the Arabic letters on the chair, and why they would not see fit to replace the chair with another one if the presence of these emblems would hurt the chair's credibility as having belonged to the Apostle Peter. If the chair really was Peter's, the pagan symbols on it must have been there before he acquired it. It would not have affected his purpose for it, if he had in fact seen and understood what the emblem of the twelve labors of Hercules was and meant, since his purpose was merely to sit on it. It is only the Church, in accordance with its propaganda of being the legitimate successor to the Nazarene movement through Peter, which considered the chair to be more than just a chair. As for the Muslim confession of faith engraved on it, the Apostle could have done it himself, since the confession of faith used by the spiritual descendants of Abraham is in full accordance with the Abrahamic Covenant made between God and Abraham: "And I will establish my covenant between me and thee and thy seed after thee in their generations for an everlasting covenant, to be a God unto thee, and to thy seed after thee" (Genensis 17:17). Again reiterated by Moses in Deuteronomy: "Hear, O Israel! The Lord our God is one Lord" (Deuternomy 6:4), and as allegorically foretold by Jesus in the thirty-ninth chapter of the gospel account compiled by the Apostle Barnabas: "Then God gave to the first man upon his thumbs that writing; upon the thumbnail of the right hand it said: "There is only one God," and upon the thumbnail of the left it said: "Muhammad is the messenger of God."

Concerning the chair and the Church's possession of the chair with its emblems and Arabic script, Sir Higgins says: "Irony aside, the fact is there is no doubt that under these mysterious circumstances, something lies hidden. These emblems and letters did not come there (to the Vatican) by accident, nor are they to be ascribed to the ignorance of the Pope and the whole college of Cardinals, and the priests of propaganda employed in educating youth in *Arabic* and other languages for the foreign missions." Continuing the subject, Higgins says: "I have read but where I cannot now recollect, and which at the time I thought of no consequence, of several missions having been sent by the Pope to convert the Caliph of the Mohammedans to Christianity. This was the ostensible reason given to the Christian world for the missions." Perhaps unaware of the existence of *The Gospel* compiled by the Apostles Matthew and Barnabas, and the familiarity of the early Gentile Church's hierarchy with that holy document and its prophecies about Muhammed, Sir Higgins goes on to say: "But I am of the opinion that these missions had also the secret object, if conversion were not possible, of effecting an accommodation; and this was in great measure caused by the expectation of a millenium, a doubt whether Mohammed might not really be the person foretold by Jesus (in John)." He states further: "We must not forget that attempts at accommodation would be kept in the most profound secrecy, and if suspected or discovered most strenuously denied — perhaps never committed to writing."[91]

In the historical episode alluded to by Higgins, one of the Popes is said to have sent an arrogant message to the Caliph to become Christian. "This story does very well," says Higgins, "to blind ignorant people, and for Protestants to Laugh at, but I believe that the truth was, that a negotiation was attempted with the Caliph by the Pope, which failed and the story of the Pope's *arrogance* was told, as we have it, to conceal the truth." Concerning this amazing episode in Christian history, Sir Higgins goes on to say: "If the Pope had any inclination to admit Mohammed as the person to be sent, as foretold by Jesus Christ, the Arabic inscription might be placed upon the chair as a preparation for a pretended miracle to establish the fact. Or if the Pope feared the arrival of the Caliph at Rome, he might be preparing for a march out to meet him with the keys of the Holy City and Heaven in his hand, with the pretence that he was at least convinced by the miraculous inscription on the chair that Mohammed was the Apostle of God."[92]

According to him, during the same time period, there seeme to have been something strangely unsettled in the Roman See. He says this is demonstrated by the fact, "now almost concealed by the priests, (he wrote in the 19th century) that a new Gospel was preached with its permission, and actively and energetically supported by it, as Mosheim says, for about thirty years. For various reasons, which will be detailed, it was at last suppressed, the zodaic and inscription on the chair were forgotten, and the Templars were burnt. The new Gospel of which I have spoken above was called the *Evangelium Eternum*, and, after being preached for some time in the 12th century, was first published in a written book by one Joachim, Abbot of Sora or Flora, in Valabria." He further states that it was called the *Book Of Joachim*. It was also known as the covenant of peace. It was intended, he says, to supersede all the old (Greek) gospels, and by way of this new gospel the Church expected a union to take place between itself and all the other sects of Christianity and the Moslem world, which caused the gospel to have the name "the covenant of peace." It also had the name *Evangelium Eternum*, or the Everlasting Gospel. "Evidently," says Higgins, "to insinuate or intimate to those capable of understanding it, that all other (Christian) gospels were only of a temporary nature."[93]

It does not matter whether the Christian world accepts the truth or not,

---

[91] Ibid.
[92] Ibid.
[93] Ibid.

their refusal is to the detriment of their own souls. Their past rejection of the most accurate account of the life and ministry of Jesus the Messiah in existence today is irrelevant, the Christian masses have been kept in the dark too long. The illegitimacy of the Christian Church's pedigree, no matter what the denomination, since they all ultimately sprang from the Nicolaitan conspiracy, nullifies its alleged qualifications to speak authoritively on the life and ministry of Jesus the Israelite Messiah. The Church is not, and never has been, the legitimate heir of the Abrahamic Covenant. Their predicament is reflected in a statement they attribute to Jesus in their New Testament: "Many will say to me in that day, Lord, Lord, have we not prophesied in Your name, cast out demons in Your name, and done many wonders in Your name? And then I will declare to them, 'I never knew you; depart from me, you who practice lawlessness' (Matthew 7:22-23). The violent, iniquitious, bigoted, unprincipled racist history of the Christian world speaks for itself.

The spiritual descendants of Abraham the friend of God, are spiritually Muslims, as that they are in the cultural and spiritual sense adherents of the "old Arabian lifestyle" of the Patriarchs: Abraham, Ishmael, Isaac, and Jacob, and the major prophets: Moses, Jesus and Muhammad. While the Christian Church and the Western world, in general, is the promoter of Graeco-Roman culture and religion with all its pagan characteristics, the true Muslims of the Muslim world are in accordance with the will of God, the promoters of the Abrahamic religion and culture in its perfected form. Graeco-Roman religion and culture are not, and never have been the continuation of the Abrahamic religion and tradition.

Believe it or not, the God of Abraham and his spiritual descendants is not the man-god of the Christians.

Appendix

LIST OF BIBLICAL AUTHORITIES

Dr. William Foxwell Albright. Professor Emeritus, former W. W. Spence professor of Semitic languages, John Hopkins University. Also member of the National Academy of Sciences (Washington), the American Philosophical Society (Philadelphia), the American Academy of Arts and Sciences (Cambridge), and the Royal Danish, Flemish, and Irish academies, the Academie des Inscriptions et Belles Lettres and of the Austrian Academy of Sciences. His list of achievements goes on.

John Marco Allegro. Born 1923, studied at the University of Manchester, and obtained a first-class Honors degree in Oriental studies in 1951. The following year he got his masters for his thesis on the linguistic background of the Balaam Oracles. He pursued further research at Oxford on Hebrew dialects. He was still at Oxford when he was asked to join the international scrolls editing team in Jerusalem as their first British representative. Until 1970, he held the post of lecturer in Old Testament and international studies at the University of Manchester.

S.G.F. Brandon. Professor of comparative religion at the University of Manchester, England.

Francis Crawford Burkitt, F.B.A., D.D. Held the post of professor of Divinity at the University of Cambridge.

Joseph Campbell, B.A., M.A. Earned his degrees at Columbia and went on to study French and Sanskrit at the University of Paris and Munich. He taught at the Canterbury School, and joined the Literature Department at Sarah Lawrence College, a post he held for many years. During the 1940's and 50's he helped Swami Nikhilananda translate the Upanishads and the gospel of Sri Ramakrishna. He has written a number of books, including *The Masks of God Occidental Mythology*.

Rev. Dr. A. Powell Davies. Author of *The Meaning of the Dead Sea Scrolls, The First Christian, America's Real Religion,* and a number of other books. He was pastor of the All Souls Church in Washington D.C., and the Community Church in Summit, N.J., before that.

Rev. Charles Harold Dodd, M.A. Professor of New Testament Greek and exegesis, Mansfield College, Oxford; lecturer in New Testament studies and Grinfield lecturer of the Septuagint at the University of Oxford.

Rev. Adam F. Findlay, M.A., D.D. Professor of Church history and Christian ethics, United Free Church College, Abardeen.

Theodor H. Gaster. Eminent Hebraist and expert on the period during which the Scrolls were written. Professor of ancient cultures at Fairleigh Dickinson University and adjunct professor of history of religions at Columbia University. He also held the post of chief of the Hebraic section in the Library of Congress and taught for many years at the Dropsie College for Hebrew and Cognate learning, Philadelphia. He has also held the post of Fullbright professor, history of religions, at the University of Rome as well as Fullbright professor, Biblical studies, at the University of Melbourne, Australia.

Godfrey Higgins, F.S.A., F.R. Born 1773, died 1833, he studied Law at Cambridge (Trinity), but upon inheriting a large fortune devoted on an average ten hours a day for nearly twenty years in search of antiquities. Author of *Anacalypsis*, a classic work on the antiquities of nations, and Celtic Druids.

Philip K. Hitti. Professor Emeritus of Semitic literature, William and Annie S. Paton Foundation Princeton University. He has earned international acclaim as a scholar, historian, and authority on the Near East. Former chairman of Princeton's Department of Oriental Studies and founder and first director of its program in Near Eastern studies. He has also held the post of lecturer at Columbia University, professor at the American university in Beirut and visiting professor at both Harvard University and the University of Sao Paulo in Brazil.

John Lewis, B.Sc., Ph.D. Lecturer in philosophy, Morley College, London, England and lecturer in anthropology, the Extra-Mural delegacy of the University of Oxford.

Gilbert Murray, M.A., D. LITT., LL.D., F.R.A. Regius professor of Greek, University of Oxford.

Margaret A. Murray, D.LIT. Fellow of University College, London.

Rev. Dr. Charles Francis Potter, B.D., S.T.M., Litt. D. Author of, *Is That In The Bible?* and *The Lost Years of Jesus Revealed*.

Samuel Sandmell. Distinguished Service professor of Bible and Hellenistic literature, Hebrew Union College-Jewish Institute of Religion.

Dr. Hugh J. Schonfield. Educated at the University of Glasgow, where he became interested in the study of the New Testament. By devoting the next forty years of his life to futher study and research, he has become a leading scholar of Biblical studies.

Rev. Charles Anderson Scott, D.D. Professor of the New Testament, Theological College of Presbyterian Church of England.

William Smith, LL.D. Compiler of the renowned *Smith's Bible Dictionary*.

INDEX

Aaron, 13, 64
Abhiras, 116
Abraham, 4, 10, 21, 22, 24, 50, 51, 56, 77, 78, 90, 109, 113, 121, 123
Abrahamic covenant, 1, 2, 10, 12, 17, 25, 111, 121, 123
Abrahamic faith, 3, 14, 50, 75, 90, 99, 108
Abrahamic religion, 2, 11, 21, 23-25, 27, 32, 34, 52, 61, 90, 91, 96, 99, 103, 111-113, 123
Achilles, 30
Acts, 71, 72, 80, 89-93
Adoptionist viewpoint, 60
Aeon, 67, 69
Agrippa, 70, 95
Age of Gentiles, 29, 30
Ahab, 21
Ahaz, 47
Ahura Mazda, 66, 85
Aingra Hainyo, 66
Albright, Foxwell, 40, 112
Alexander, 3, 29-31, 36, 116
Alexanderia, 31, 94, 97
Alke-bulan, 29, 35
Alkebulani, 30
Allegro, John, 50
Ammon, 65
Amos, 4, 22
Anacalypsis, 110
Ananias, 64, 88
Anastasius, Emperor, 81, 82
Anatolian, 2

Ancient of Days, 106
Andrew, 11, 13, 26, 88
Angels, 16
Angel of the Lord, 18
Antinomians, 48
Antioch, 90, 91, 93
Antiochian, 93
Antiochus, IV 31, 43
Antiochus, Epiphanes, 3, 4
Aphrodite, 51
Apollo, 65
Apostle, 72, 101
Apostles, 50, 70, 76, 77, 79, 90
Apostolic, 55, 91, 95, 97
Apostolic congregation, 48, 50, 56, 72
Arab, 4, 21, 22, 112
Arabs, 4
Arabia, 2, 17, 70, 74, 111, 112, 115
Arabian, 2, 4, 96, 112, 113
Arabians, 115
Arabic, 2, 118, 120-122
Aramic, 5, 79
Aristotle, 30
Aryan, 66
Asceticism, 10
Asia, 29
Asian, 30
Assyrian, 105
Assyrians, 21, 28
Astyages, 29
Atonement, day of 4

130 Index

Augustine, St. 83, 119
Augustus Caesar, 15, 21, 36
Aurantis, 108
Avesta, 66

Baal, 21, 23, 51
Babylon, 32
Babylonia, 29, 31
Babylonian, 2, 28
Babylonians, 21
Balaam, 48
Balkh, 115
Bar-cochba, 108
Barnabas, 3, 5, 8, 9, 60, 70, 71, 75, 79, 87, 89, 91-94, 97, 101, 106, 110, 121
Barnabas, acts of, 89, 94, 116
Barnabas, Gospel of, 5, 6, 11-13, 16, 17, 19, 24-26, 37-40, 44, 47, 48, 60, 61, 72, 87,-89, 91, 96, 100, 107, 109, 110, 113-115, 118, 119
Barnabe, Evangelium, 101
Bar-jesus, 89, 91, 92
Bartholomew, 88, 94, 116
Bashan, 1
Bedawi, 2
Berlzebub, 36
Belshazzar, 32
Benedictine monks, 81, 82
Bethlehem, 15-18
Bethlehem of Ephrath, 105
Berry, Gerald, 66, 79,
Bible, 2, 14, 22, 40
Biblical, 31
Bishop Marsh, 118
Book of Haggi, 110, 113
Book of Hymns, 7
Book of Joachim, 122
Bozrah, 106
Brandon, S.G.F., 68, 76, 79, 80
Britain, 35
Burkitt, Francis Crawford, 84

Caesar, 16, 33
Caesar, Julius, 21, 27, 33, 35, 36
Caesarea, 40, 96

Caiaphas, 15
Caliph, 121, 122
Cambyses, 29
Canaanite, 21, 42, 61
Canaanites, 13, 50
Capernum, 39
Cardinals, College of, 121
Canterbury, 82
Catholic, 72
Catholic Church, 55, 83
Cephas, 71, 77
Cerinthus, 85
Christ, 42, 76, 79
Christian(s), 56, 60, 61, 68, 79-83, 88, 94, 98, 104, 109, 116, 121, 123
Christiandom, 116
Christianity, 12, 63, 68, 81, 82, 84, 85, 94, 97, 99, 101, 121, 122
Christian Church, 89, 97, 99, 101, 108, 116, 120, 123,
Christian religion, 82, 101
Christian religion scriptures, 82
Christian religion scholars, 11
Church, 76, 82-84, 94, 95, 104, 116, 121
Church Fathers, 82, 89
Cilicia, 70
Cleanthes, 62
Clement of Alexandria, 98
Clementines, 101, 119
Comforter, 117, 118
Confraternity version of Bible, 55
Constantinople, 81, 82, 120
Corinthians I, 99, 53, 56, 72
Corinthians, 54, 69
Corinthians II, 72, 76
Covenant, 4, 24, 46, 112
Crassus, 36
Cromus, 51
Cyaxares, 28, 29
Cyrene, 90
Cyprus, 89, 90, 94
Cyrus, 29

Damascus, 1, 4, 61-65, 69, 74
Damascus Document, 1, 4

Damascus Road, 70
Daniel, 4, 28, 32, 33, 95, 105
Danube, 29
Davies, A. Powell, 7, 69, 70, 71
David, 9, 12, 14, 16, 24, 26, 78, 103, 104, 105, 109, 113, 114
Dea Myrionymus, 66
Dead Sea Scrolls, 59
Decapolis, 1, 96
December 25th, 51 (birthday of the Pagan gods)
Decretium Gelansium, 101
Demetrius, Bishop of Alexandria, 116
Demonsthenes, 29
Destiny, 67
Deuteronomic Law, 23
Diaspora, 31
Dionusos, 65
Dionysius, Bishop of Corinith, 79, 81
Disciples, 25, 41
Doctors, 37
Dodd, Charles Harold, 97

Earth, 66
Earth-mother goddess, 51
Ebion, 61
Ebionites, 60-64, 87, 92
Edom, 106
Edomite, 106
Egypt, 2, 13-18, 29, 34, 35, 46, 51, 67, 82, 105
Egyptian, 2, 3, 53, 65, 116
Elect of Israel, 4
Elijah, 10, 21, 38, 41, 46, 105, 110
Elisha, 21
Elymas, 91
Emperor Domition, 108
Emperor Flavius Theodosius, 101
Emperor Valentinian III, 101
Emperor Vespasian, 103
Emperor Zeno, 94
English, 55, 117
Emoch, 38
Ephesians, 35

Epirus, 29
Epistles, 99, 100
Epistle to the Galatians, 76
Epistle to the Hebrews, 42, 100
Epistle to the Romans, 56, 101, 119
Era of wickedness, 107
Esaias, 110
Essean, 5
Essene, 26, 87, 104
Essenes, 4, 5, 7, 9, 12, 14, 24, 26, 50, 51, 90, 108
Essene movement, 1, 3, 5, 59, 60
Essenic, 90, 106, 107
Essenic Book of Hymns, 6
Essenic movement, 4, 9, 27
Essenic Teachers, 27
Europe, 29, 82
Eusebius, 103, 104
Evangelum Eternum, 122
Eve, 76
Ezekiel, 24, 106, 112

Fertility cults, 23
Findlay, Adam, F.
Florus, 96
Form, 66
Fourth gospel, 85
Fourth kingdom, 95
Fra Marino, 119
French, 120

Gabriel, 9, 15, 39, 41, 60, 114
Galatians, 56, 63, 65, 70-73, 74, 75, 77
Galilee, 1, 15, 18, 38, 41, 60, 80, 96, 105, 108
Galileans II, 96, 105
Gallus, 96
Garnier, Col. J., 66, 68, 116
Gaster, Theodor H.
Gaul, 35
Gaulan, I
Gaulantis, 108
Genesis, 2, 22, 27
Gentile(s), 3, 11, 14, 21, 24, 27,

28, 30, 33, 35-37, 42, 48-51, 55, 56, 61, 62, 65, 69, 70, 72, 74, 75, 77, 78, 82, 85, 93, 94, 96, 98, 99, 100, 117
Gentile church, 79, 99, 119, 120
Gentile gospels, 81, 83
Gentile misconcerption of divinity, 41, 46-47
Germany, 36
Gibraltar, 29
Gilrad, 1
Gnostic, 48, 53-56, 66-68, 85, 90, 97-99, 110
Gnostics, 50
Gnosticism, 42, 66, 68, 69, 97
God (works in man), 46
God fearers, 61, 62, 89
Golden age, 105
Goodspeed, 55
Gospel(s), 3, 8, 26, 48, 61, 74, 79, 80, 82, 84, 87-89, 93, 101, 103, 104, 115, 116, 119, 122
Gospels, Synoptic, 79
Gospel of Jesus, 5, 50, 56, 79, 81, 89, 91, 92, 100, 108
Gospel of John, 41, 42, 53, 80, 83, 84, 118
Gospel of Luke, 80, 83, 84, 94
Gospel of Mark, 83, 84
Gospel of Matthew, 80, 83, 84
Goyim, 27
Graeco, 2, 96
Graeco-Roman, 2, 95, 123
Greece, 30, 33, 35, 51, 52
Greek(s), 5, 7, 29, 30-36, 51,-53, 61-63, 65, 67, 79, 89, 95, 99, 100, 117
Greek church, 51
Grollenberg, 29, 31

Hagar, 64
Haggi, 110
HMD, 110
Hasideans, 3
Hasidim, 10
Hasmoneans, 3

Hauran, 1
Heaven, 66
Hebrew, 62, 89, 94, 106, 115, 116
Hebrews, 2, 43, 104
Hellas, 30
Hellenic, 31
Hellenist(s), 3, 70, 90
Hellenistic, 90
Hellenism, 2, 3, 10, 34
Hellenized, 3, 29, 50, 87
Hellenization, 3, 31, 37, 43
Hellenized Jews, 31, 32, 43, 48, 90, 91
Hera, 51
Heracleon, 84
Hercules, 30, 65, 120, 121
Hermes, 65
Hermetic, 65, 66, 85
Hermetic writers, 98
Herod, 15, 17, 18, 43, 45, 46, 91
Higgins, Godfrey, 65, 81-83, 110, 118-122
Hindi, 116
Hindus, 66
Hitti Philip k., 23
Holy Angel, 44
Holy beings, 6
Holy one of God, 9, 87
Holy Spirit, 36, 47, 51, 54-56
Homilies, 88
Homeric songs, 30
Horeb, 112

Ibhri (Hebrew), 116
Ikmal ad-Din, 115
Illumination of the heart, 59-60
Illustrious, 118
Illyrian, 33
Immanuel, 47
Isaac, 4, 51, 56, 78, 113, 114
Isaiah, 11, 13, 14, 23, 24, 47, 106
Iscariot, Judas, 88
Ishmael, 1, 4, 51, 56, 113, 114
Ishmaelite, 2, 4, 40, 111
Ishmaelites, 4, 10, 21-24, 112,

113
Isis, 67
Israel, 2, 4, 9, 13, 15, 17, 22-24, 46, 90, 95, 105, 107, 109, 111, 112
Israelite, 1, 21, 22, 27, 40, 50, 90, 106
Israelites, 2, 23, 42, 56, 64, 89, 91, 105, 108, 111, 112
Israelite dispensation, 25
Israelite Messiah, 61
Italy, 33, 120

Jacob, 4, 51, 56, 95, 113
James, 13, 26, 70-72, 74, 88, 103, 113
James the just, 77, 91, 96, 101
Japheth, 27, 28
Japhethinans, 28, 66
Jehonadab, 21
Jehu, 21, 112
Jeremiah, 1, 4, 23, 24, 40, 110
Jericho, 1
Jerome, 94
Jerusalem, 3, 4, 17-19, 23, 24, 31, 37, 38, 40, 44, 62, 70, 71, 74, 80, 88, 90-92, 95, 96, 98, 99, 103, 105
Jesus, 1, 3, 7-19, 24-27, 35-40, 42-48, 54, 56, 59-61, 64, 68, 69, 71, 72, 75, 77-80, 83, 88, 90, 91, 93-97, 100-109
Jethro, 4, 113
Jews, 1, 3, 4, 8, 9, 14, 17, 24, 27, 34, 37, 61, 62, 74, 90, 95, 96, 103,-106, 113
Jews, (corrupted scripture) 14
Jewish, 3, 4, 22, 31, 34, 56, 63, 88, 93, 95-99, 108
Jewish avthorities, 68
Jewish converts, 50
Jewish nationalism, 103
Jewish sanhedrin, 90
Jewish scriptures, 62
Jewish scriptures (essenic and argument against), 12
Jewish (corruption of scriptures), 104
Joachim, 122
John, 26, 42, 77, 79, 85, 88, 90
John the Baptist, 1, 60, 61
John I, 84
Jonah, 14
Jordan, 96
Jordan river, 44, 46, 60, 96
Joseph, 13-16, 18, 19, 103, 105
Josephus, 7, 95
Joshua, 46, 114
Juasaph, 115
Jubilers, 107
Judah, 9, 15, 17, 23, 31, 43, 47, 105, 113
Judaic, 2, 59, 88
Judaism, 3, 50, 61, 74
Judas, 88
Jude, 103
Judea, 15, 17, 18, 29, 31, 39, 44, 45, 70, 71, 90, 109, 110
Judean, 71, 104
Judean bethlehem, 105
Juno, 116
Jupiter, 65, 116
Justin, 84
Justus, 104
Kashmir, 115
Kenites, 22
Keturah, 22
King James version of Bible, 27, 55
King Josiah, 23
Kingdom of David, 50
Kingdom of Heaven, 105
Lamech, 117
Lanfranc, 81, 82
Last days, 50, 108
Latins, 33
Latin church, 99
Lebanon, 1
Lebbacus, 89
Leo, 116
Levi, 22, 106
Levites, 22, 110

Logos, 85, 98
Lord of glory, 100
Lucius of Cyrene, 91
Luke, 79, 96
Lydda, 96
Lydia, 29

Maccabees, 3, 31
Maccabean, 4, 31,43
Macedonians, 29
Madianites, 13
Magi, 17, 85
Magianism, 66
Manaean, 91
Manual of Discipline, 5, 6, 8, 59, 60, 104, 106
Marius, 33, 35
Mark, 79, 91-93, 96
Mary, 9, 10, 15-19, 60, 109
Martha, 41
Matter, 66
Matthai, 88
Matthew, 3, 5, 8, 11, 42, 48, 60, 78, 79, 88, 89, 94-96, 101, 104, 106, 116, 121
Matthias, 3, 116
Meek, Theophile J., 113
Median dynasty, 28
Median Empire, 28, 29
Medo-Persian Empire, 28
Melchizdek, 56
Memoirs of Hegesippus, 109
Messala, 81
Messapians, 33
Messenger, 117, 118
Messiah, 17, 24, 41, 50, 69, 75, 89, 95, 105-107, 109, 110, 113-115, 117, 118
Midianites, 22
Mithra, 65, 67, 85
Moab, 95
Moffat, 55
Muhammed, 110, 114, 118, 121, 122, 129
Mohammedans, 121
Momotheists, 27

Monotheism vs Dualism, 55
Monotheism vs Trinitarianism, 40, 55
Moon, 66
Mosaic law, 2, 4, 15, 17, 48, 56, 61, 89, 100
Moses, 2, 4, 11, 13, 19, 27, 39, 41, 44, 46, 48, 50, 64, 109, 112-114, 121
Moses, (book of) 26
Mosheim, 122
Mount Olivet, 59
Mount of Olives, 105
Mount Tabor, 105
Mount Sinai, 17, 44
Murray, Gilbert, 52
Murray, Margaret, 53
Muslim (Moslem), 120, 122
Muslims, 123
Nain, 38, 39
Nathaniel, 41
Nazarene, 5, 64, 75, 87, 90, 92, 101-104, 106, 108, 121
Nazarenes, 9, 12, 27, 48, 49, 57, 60, 61, 91, 93, 96-100, 109, 113, 116
Nazarene Gospel Restored, 62
Nazarene Movement, 1, 3, 72, 115
Nazareth, 15, 18, 19
Nazarites, 10, 22
Nebuchadnezzar, 28, 29, 32, 33
Negeb, 112
Nephthys, 67
Nero, 98
New Testament, 24, 70-72, 79-81, 83, 87, 89, 93, 94, 96-99, 117, 123
Nicolaitan, 3, 65, 66, 69, 74, 77, 81, 82, 90, 91, 94, 103, 120, 123
Nicolaitans, 48, 50-53, 55-57, 61, 68, 72, 75, 79, 85, 89, 92, 93, 98-100, 104, 108, 116
Nicolaitan Church of Rome, 109
Nielsen, Ditlef, 2
Nile, 29

Noah, 117
Nochian laws, 27
Nonnus, 65
Old Testamen, 42, 62, 112
Omphis, 65
Oral tradition, 62
Oracles in Hebrew, 105
Orphic, 52, 67
Oscans, 33
Osiris, 51, 53, 65, 67
Osirian, 53

Paganism, 52
Pakistan, 29, 30
Palestine, 3, 5, 10, 61, 97, 115
Pamphylia, 92
Pan, 65
Pantaenus, 94, 97, 116
Paphos, 91
Papias, 89
Paraclete, 117-119
Paradise, 7
Parkhurst III,
Parsi scripture, 115
Parsis, 115
Passover, 40
Patera, 117
Patriarchs, 2, 4, 10, 16, 60
Paul, 3, 49, 50, 53, 56, 57, 61, 62, 64, 65, 68-70, 72, 74,-77, 79, 81, 89, 91-93, 99-101, 119
Pauline theology, 100
Paulus, Sergius, 89, 91, 92
Pekah, 48
Pella, 96, 97, 99
Penitents, 1, 2, 4
Pentateuch, 62
Perga, 92
Periclyte, 118
Persia, 29, 36, 115
Persian, 17, 29, 66
Persian Gulf, 106
Peter, 41, 70, 74, 88, 90, 100, 101, 119-121
Pethor, 48
Pharaoh, 13, 46

Pharisees, 12, 37
Pharsalus, 35
Philadelphus, 31
Philemon, 72
Philip, 88
Philip of Macedonia, 30
Philippi, 40
Phillipians, 72
Philo, 98
Phoenicia, 90
Picentes, 33
Pilate, 15, 43
Pious remnants, 1
Plato, 52
Platonic, 67
Pluto, 65
Poimandres, 85
Pompey, 35
Pompius, 98
Pope(s), 82, 120-121
Pope Clement X, 120
Pope Damasus, 101
Pope Sixtus V, 119
Potter, Charles F., 51, 55
Presbyter Gaius, 84
Prophets, 1, 10, 13, 16, 42, 62, 77
Protestant(s), 72, 82, 83, 122
Psalter of Solomon, 105
Ptolemaeus, 84
Ptolemies, 31, 53
Ptolemy II, 31

Qur'an, 27
Qumran, 4, 50, 51, 61
Qumran Community, 1, 4, 5, 7, 72
Qumran Scrolls, 1, 5, 48, 87
Quelle ("Q" = source), 94

Rabbi, 41
Rabbi Gamaliel, 62
Rabbinic sources, 106
Rachel, 18
Rahab, 78
Ramah, 18
Rechabites, 1, 4, 10, 22, 24, 112

Recognitions, 88
Rigveda, 66
Rehoboam, 105
Religion, 2
Revelation, 48
Rezin, king of Damascus, 48
Rheims version of Bible, 55
Rhine, 36
Rome, 30, 33, 35, 36, 82, 95-98, 100, 101, 120, 122
Roman, 96, 99, 103, 108, 116
Romans, 32, 34-36, 39, 68, 77, 88, 95, 96, 98, 104, 106
Roman Character, 33
Roman Christianity, 101
Roman Church, 84, 99, 100
Roman Empire, 32
Roman soldiery, 37, 43, 91
Roman tradition, 101
Roman see, 122
Ruth, 14
Ryland's library, 84

Sabbath, 3, 4
Sabines, 33
Samaria, 90
Salamis, 89
Sale, George, 118, 119
Satan, 25, 36, 39, 41, 43-46, 48, 75, 99, 109, 113
Saul (Paul), 63, 64, 90, 91
Saternia (Saturnia), 33
Saturn, 116
Savior, 67, 69
Scillitan Christians, 100
Scott, Charles Anderson, 79, 84
Scribes, 12, 17, 37, 110
Scriptures, 24, 31, 34, 36, 95, 106
Sythian, 28
Sedillot, Rene, 29, 30
Seluecid dynasty, 3
Semitic, 3, 27
Semites, 2
Senate (Roman), 35
Shepherds, 16
Sibyline oracles, 105

Sinai, 10, 112
Siculus, Diodorus, 65
Simeon son of Cleophas, 103, 104
Siris, 65
Smith, William, 10, 47, 48, 50, 56, 98, 100, 112, 119
Sokker, 103
Solomon, 21, 36, 42, 47
Song of songs, 14
Spain, 35
Spirit of God, 60
Spirit of Truth, 117, 118
Stephen, 65, 90, 91
Sulla, 35
Sun, 66, 117
Symeon, 91
Synagogue Judaism, 34
Synoptic gospels, 79
Syria, 3, 34, 61, 70, 116
Syriac, 118
Syrian, 70

Tacitus, 33
Talmud, 27
Targum of Onkelos, 95
Tarikh A'azami, 115
Taus, 115
Temple of the Lord, 3, 23, 90, 95
Terramare, 33
Testament of Levi, 106
Thaddaeus, 89
The Elect, 5
The Elect of God, 5, 6
Thoth, 65
Thrace, 29
Thessalonians, I 72
Tobias, 31
Torah, 1, 7, 14
Trojan, 30
Trans-Jordan, 31, 61
Trinity, 48, 51, 55, 56
Tununensis, Victor, 81

Umbrians, 33
Vatican, 120, 121

Western Asia, 82

Yahweh, 23, 112
Yuz Asaf, 115

Zeus, 30, 52
Zebedee, 53
Zadokite document, 106